ESCOGIDO RXV: THE CHOSEN

SALLIE A. STEWART

with

PJ LOWERY, ANNIE LUBINSKI & DARYL LUBINSKI

Edited by Pamela Krueger

Cover Photo by Charles Hilton

Dedicated to Desiree Bruce

CONTENTS

SALLIE A. STEWART

ACKNOWLEDGMENTS

Special thanks to
Debbie Brown
Tracey Goforth
Gretchen Schroeder
Gramps

FORWARD

March 2015

"You may encounter many defeats, but you must not be defeated. In fact, it may be necessary to encounter the defeats, so you can know who you are, what you can rise from, how you can still come out of it."

—Maya Angelou

While we most often associate our hearts with love and feeling, it is our brain that is at the core of what makes us human. Weighing just three pounds and containing some 100 billion neurons, it is responsible for a staggering number of functions—from mundane motor tasks like how to load the dishwasher to the more profound, like encoding, storing and recalling information and recognizing our friends and family.

On the face of it, this is a book about tragedy and chance, about the fragility of existence and one woman's determination to overcome insurmountable challenges. Sallie Stewart's remarkable account embraces all those things, but more than anything, it is a story about love: that between husband and wife and mother and son. It shows us that rehabilitation can come from unexpected places, and how the extraordinary bond between Sallie and her horse facilitated her healing.

I first spoke to Sallie when I was writing an article about head injuries for Dressage Today magazine. The equestrian world had been seriously shaken in 2010, when American Olympic dressage rider Courtney King-Dye sustained a skull fracture and a traumatic brain injury after the young horse she was riding tripped and fell. Dressage riders discovered that even in our seemingly low-risk sport, any one of us could suffer a head injury, and a movement promoting the use of helmets picked up speed.

Over and over, I studied the details of Sallie's accident, searching for reasons why it had occurred and what other riders and athletes could take away from it. The sheer randomness of it was especially chilling: It was a beautiful day, the footing in her arena was good, she was an experienced rider on a horse she knew well, there was no precipitating factor—no sudden gust of wind, no loud noise. Her horse went down, and her life changed forever. Sallie articulated the experience with great passion, but made it clear she'd never be the person she was before. "A traumatic brain injury is not a one-time event that you heal from," she told me. "It's a lifelong deal."

A continuing bright light on her continuing journey to heal and rediscover herself came from the extraordinary support provided by the two "Michaels" in Sallie's life—her husband, Michael, who stood by her even when she had no idea who he was or why she'd married him and who also urged her to tell her story, and her coach, dressage judge and trainer Mike Osinski, who had a remarkable sense of just when and how to encourage her both on horseback and off, and when to hold back.

For the estimated 1.7 million children and adults who suffer traumatic brain injuries each year and their families, life is often divided into two parts: before the accident and after. That Sallie Stewart is able to share her story is nothing short of a miracle. That she has made it a mission to reach out to fellow equestrians who've suffered a TBI tells something deeper about the kind of person she is.

Kelly Vencill Sanchez
Glendale, CA

SALLIE A. STEWART

2008

SALLIE A. STEWART

CHAPTER ONE
Life Deals Us All A Hand

"If one dream should fall and break into a thousand pieces, never be afraid to pick up on of those pieces and begin again"
~Flavia Weedn

February 17th 2008 was a beautiful spring day. It was the kind of day where you remember why you live in the State of Washington. The sun was out; the sky was a brilliant deep blue. The evergreen trees were magically green in contrast to the bare leaved white oaks. And Mt Rainier towered majestically against the blue background, stark and white, in all her glory.

As Sallie got up and got dressed, Michael her husband let her know he would be working on finishing the fencing on the farm. After getting dressed, she saw Chayce, her 12 year old son, at the kitchen table along with her girlfriend, Jenny, who was there to ride also. "Good morning mom! Can I go play at Ian's? The sun is out and we want to finish our fort." She peered out the kitchen window that over looked the arena. The sunlight on the sand just glistened! She answered to Chayce, "Sure. Why don't you do that.....sounds like a great time". The young boy shouted out "Yeah! Thanks mom. Hey what are you going to do today?" Sallie smiled while she patted Chayce on the head and gave him a kiss, "With a day like today? Ride of course!". Chayce finished breakfast and ran out the door, with Sallie saying, "Don't slam the door and be home before dark!" Chayce answered, "I will" as the door slammed shut behind him. Sallie laughed as she thought, "Well he got half of it right."

Sallie and Jenny both laughed at Chayce's enthusiasm. Jenny said, "So I will meet you down there?" Sallie replied with a head nod and told her, "Yes meet you down there. Just have a phone call to make."

Sallie's oldest son had been on her mind as he was away at college. She made a phone call to check in with him, "Yes mom?" Rian answered. "Hey son, how are you? Classes going ok?" Rian answered, "Its college mom; classes are hard." Sallie responded, "I know kiddo. But, you can do it. You can." Rian answered, "How would you know?" Sallie, used to the lack of respect, answered, "Hey I took classes at a community college." Rian responded, "That does not even compare." Sallie cut off the debate, telling Rian "Son, I did not call to argue with you. I called to see how you are. I love you and you sound good. Keep in touch. And I am so glad you have the opportunity to attend a four year university." Rian answered, "Love you too mom" followed with a 'click" of the phone. Sallie thought to herself, "Yep…eighteen…have all the answer…parents are idiots. I get it."

Sallie walked down the hill to the barn and the arena. She noticed Michael working on the fence and walked over to him…gave him a gentle kiss on the lips. His hands were busy with wire and fence posts, but he still took the time to lock eyes with hers, bringing a smile to each of their faces. Michael asked, "You going riding?" Sallie glanced over at Esco standing in his paddock, "Yes what a day for it! It's so beautiful!". Michael glanced at Esco as well. "Have a great ride babe!" She reached up and gave him her usual warm hug. Then Sallie made her way to catch up Esco. "Come on buddy." She said to Esco, who clearly understood, as he followed her while she strode the outside on his fence line, and the two met in his stall. She began tacking him up in the cross ties in the tack area. The rope on either side of him was attached to a post, keeping him steady, so she could brush his body and put the saddle on. Jenny was already riding her horse in the arena. Sallie noticed Esco's attention was not on her. He fidgeted, tossing his head and stomping his feet. "Esco…hey! Hey you stay here. Esco……whoa! You stand." she said as she lifted each hoof and picked his feet and, finally, put his saddle on and inched the girth up until it was snug.

Due to Esco's obvious lack of focus, he kept moving his feet and tossing his head, looking around at every little distraction, Sallie decided she needed to lunge him to assure his focus was on the job at hand. While lunging him in the arena, she noticed Esco was not paying attention to her cues at all. He kept tripping over his own feet. He seemed more focused, still, on the other horse in the arena and the noises Michael was making at the fence. There was no explosion, no bouncing around on Esco's part. It was nothing noticeable to anyone but Sallie. She just knew Esco was not paying attention to her. "Hey"…..she said to her friend, "It's not our day. Go ahead and ride without us. Sallie had always been good a reading Esco's energy, and something just didn't feel right. He …..he's just not ready to go on a hack today." Her friends said, "What's he doing? He looks fine to me?" Again, Sallie said, "No…I just don't have his attention to day." The friend laughed and said, "The only thing stopping you is fear itself. Come on….lets go." Sallie laughed. Being that Esco had not bucked, blown up or was being a monster, she thought…" well maybe I need to just go. Must be in my head." So, she walked Esco to the mounting block, and as she mounted Esco, she said, "Hey….if anything happens today, I just want to let you know I am kicking your ass!" Both girls laughed.

5

Michael continued working on the west side of the property. He was putting in a new perimeter fence on a hill overlooking the arena and barn. From this vantage point, he watched Sallie mount Esco, and the horse and rider began walking along the west rail to the north end of the arena. He was back to work, but looked up again when he heard Sallie yell. As a trained police officer, Michael's attention was naturally drawn to anything out of the ordinary, and this caught his attention immediately. He strained to see exactly what was happening. He could see Esco through the fence railing, but Sallie had disappeared. Intuitively, he knew something was wrong and moved quickly toward the corner of the fence. Sallie yelled again.

Now Michael saw the problem—Esco had stopped, and his front feet were crossed. As he watched with horror, the horse's knees buckled and started to shake. Before he could react, Michael saw the horse begin to tip, and in the next moment, the stallion disappeared) below view. Michael heard a thud as the horse hit the compact sand with Sallie beneath him. Taking off at a dead run, Michael raced toward the arena. Within moments, he found Esco laying on his right side, but no Sallie. Where was she?   Then he realized that Esco had fallen on his right side on top of Sallie, so Michael hadn't seen her at first.

Both Mike and Esco knew something was wrong. Instead of scrambling to his feet, Esco leaned to his left and lifted up his head. When Esco saw Sallie lying at his right side, he immediately threw his weight to his left, away from her. Esco did everything he could not to roll on her and not to hurt her any further. The horse lunged up onto his feet and walked away from Sallie. She lay crumpled on her right side with her chin tucked in tight. In that moment all Michaels training took over, even while his heart was in his throat. "Call an ambulance!" he shouted to Jenny.

Michael realized that Sallie was not breathing and was making a gurgling sound. It was apparent that she was laboring hard to breathe with her chin tucked down. Michael braced her neck with his hand and tipped her head back, opening her airway. He turned her on her back, placed his mouth over hers, and gave her a couple of quick puffs of breath. She was limp and pale. Her eyes were closed, and her mouth was slack. He continued to work to help her breathe. Suddenly, she gasped and her body began seizing. All Michael could do was keep her airway open and hold her seizing form. He lay next to her, trying to hold her still. He checked her body for broken bones, but did not feel any. He whispered to her softly, telling her help was on the way. She was breathing on her own, but she was unconscious, and her body continued seizing until the medics arrived.

Esco walked to the opposite end of the arena when the ambulance arrived. He peered at Michael and Sallie from a distance, head down, nickering occasionally. Sallie continued to seize as the emergency response team worked feverishly to stabilize her in the arena. They settled her on a body board, strapped her in, and then lifted her into the ambulance. After several minutes, Michael finally heard her moan. That was the first sound he had heard from her in several minutes, but it gave Michael little comfort. Intuitively, he knew this wasn't good.

The ambulance rushed Sallie to Providence St. Peter Hospital in Olympia, Washington. Chayce, their 12 year old, was already at the neighbors, so Michael phoned to make sure Chayce could stay with them for the night, and informed them that Sallie had had an accident on her horse. Michael's responses to the incident at that point were automatic. Police officers are trained to observe first, then to follow steps to secure the situation and react to the immediate needs of the moment. Immediately he began to handle, without emotion, the necessary details. Then he hurried to the emergency room to see her.

When he arrived at the emergency room, Michael was told that Sallie had been already taken from the emergency room and sent for a brain scan. A nurse led him to a waiting room where he sat and waited, appearing to be completely composed, as was his training. Actually, he was deep in thought, trying to reconstruct the scene of the accident. Lost in his thoughts, it seemed like only moments when the surgeon came through the door. The doctor was cold and firm. He told Michael that Sallie had a concussion and a few brain bleeds. He explained they would perform a second scan in six hours to determine whether the bleeding had stopped. Continuing with his assessment, the doctor told Michael they were giving Sallie a heavy dose of several medications to help stop the bleeding and swelling in her brain. He explained that, if the bleeding did not stop, Sallie would need to undergo surgery to alleviate the pressure building in her skull. Michael was relieved when he was met again by the neurologist, who told him the second CT scan showed that the bleeding had stopped. There was no mention of further injuries, nor the significance of inner cranial brain bleeds, so for Michael, it seemed the worst might be over.

It was late, around 9 or 10 p.m. Feeling some relief, Michael went to grab some dinner. As he was eating at a restaurant just across the street from the hospital, Michael was surprised to get a call from Sallie. And she sounded fine—for about a minute. Then, suddenly, her speech became slurred and garbled, and he couldn't understand her. In that moment Michael was reminded that his wife was not yet out of the woods, though he could not yet realize this was a harbinger of a much greater struggle to come for everyone.

He made a couple of phone calls, one to Sallie's grandfather and one to her mother. He told them Sallie had had an accident. Her horse had fallen on her, and they were at the hospital. She wasn't on life support or anything, but that the doctors were watching. She had a couple of brain bleeds, and if the bleeding didn't stop in six hours, she would have to have brain surgery. And then he said, "…but it's alright, it's alright, she is going to be just fine." It was a little bit like he was trying to convince himself. He was still in shock and in a state of disbelief.

Once finished with his dinner and the phone calls, Mike returned to the hospital and   learned that Sallie had been placed in the Intensive Care Unit. But he didn't find her in her bed in the ICU. Instead, he found her staggering down the hallway using a handrail to support herself. It was obvious that she was not able to stand on her own and seemed disoriented. He helped her walk her back to her bed. At that point a nurse arrived and reprimanded Michael that Sallie couldn't be out of bed. Michael shook his head in disbelief.

Meanwhile, Michael's phone was ringing. Friends were calling to tell him that Sallie had been calling them. "She isn't making any sense," they said. She had apparently been making lots of phone call, so Michael instructed the nurses to take the phone out of her room. Confident that Sallie was in good hands and hoping that the worst was over, he drove, exhausted, back to the farm to care for the horses and get some much needed sleep.

Sallie remained in the hospital for four days and three nights, and if she could speak one day, she couldn't the next. If she could walk one day, the next day she could not move.

On the morning following the accident, Michal returned to Sallie's room. The moment he walked into the hospital room, Michael realized something was very wrong. Sallie told him from her bed that she had just made coffee, had folded the blankets, had done the laundry, all things that Michael knew hadn't happened. Yet, it was clear that she could not even get out of bed. Her balance and coordination was so poor, but he took consolation in the fact that he hadn't found her stumbling down the hallway.

Sallie remained in ICU for a couple of days, before she was transferred into the neurology unit. Sallie fell asleep as they moved her bed and woke up to find herself in a single room with large bay windows. She thought she was in a hotel room.

When Mike returned to visit her that day, she scolded Michael about renting such an expensive hotel room, "because we can't afford it," were the words she slurred. "We're not in a hotel room, we're in the hospital," Michael told her, but Sallie seemed to be trapped somewhere in space and time. Michael tried to balance his concern with a belief that all this would pass in time.

But time was not the only issue for Sallie. It took much longer for Sallie and Michael to begin to understand the extent of her injuries. Not until two years after the accident would they come to learn she had something called a Traumatic Brain injury. No discussion was initiated by her doctors about facial fractures, including a fractured eye socket and a crushed disk in her jaw, or about a traumatic brain injury. The discharge papers from the initial hospital stay simply stated "concussion." They would also come to learn, much later, that she had injured several cranial nerves.

At the time of the accident, the hospital staff hadn't told Michael much either. After Sallie spent a final night in the neurology unit, they told Michael she could go home. He was a bit shocked by that, as it was obvious that Sallie could not speak well, could not walk without his assistance, and felt very nauseated. The staff told him Sallie needed to follow-up with her primary care physician and that she would be better in time. There was, again, no explanation of the extent of her injuries or what to expect of "recovery". Michael was extremely confused with the reality of her imminent release. He realized that Sallie was still much disoriented, had no balance, could speak only a few slurred words at a time, and had the voice of a five year old. In fact, she appeared worse now than she had just two days before. However, he found himself intuitively trusting the opinions of those who were caring for Sallie. Surely doctors, much like police officers and firefighters, knew their job and shouldn't be questioned. As the days passed, Michael realized the person he had known as a generous nurturer and fierce fighter had changed completely. The woman who he had counted on to help him load hay, do farm chores, take care of the household, cook; the professional woman who he admired for her career in financing and banking, could no longer balance herself when standing on her feet. She became so dizzy when she moved that she was incapable of getting off the couch. Her jaw constantly hurt and she developed a difficulty chewing. Michael now found himself having to prepare and feed his wife a soft food diet to ensure she maintained the little strength that she still possessed. He had to help her get up, use the bathroom, dress and function in general. His intensely independent, fireball of a wife was now a twenty-four hour responsibility. The woman, who could hold her own in any argument, could no longer remember words or how to form them.

There was no conversation between the family members. Rian, the oldest son was away at college and unaware of what had been happening.

Then, the greatest challenge they would face as a family came to bare. The man Sallie now had caring for her was a stranger, her children were unfamiliar, and perhaps worst of all, she no longer knew who she was. She had no memory of being married or having children, friends, or a job. The effect of this new-found reality was terrifying to her, for she knew not what had happened to bring it on.

Simultaneously, her mental anguish, brought on from her missing memories, became intense. Additionally, Sallie was becoming increasingly limited in her physical abilities. It was not unusual for the phone to ring, though Sallie was oblivious to the noise. She frequently found herself unable to move from the couch, which had now become her bed, and standing up was particularly difficult. Often she would find herself unable to sit steady or raise herself up without Michael's help. Even after using the assistance of another person to rise up, Sallie would have to stop and wait for the flash of vertigo to pass before she would need further assistance to where she wanted to go. So great were the challenges posed by this injury, that Sallie could not even accomplish the most basic of functions, such as using a bathroom, without needing Michael's assistance. Even then, Sallie often found herself unable to communicate her need for help. Instead, Michael learned to rely on his intuition to tell him when she might need his assistance. Overnight, Michaels whole being had become one with Sallie and Chayce. His life had changed from that of full time police officer as to include the job as the exclusive caretaker for the two people he loved the most. Adding to the ever-growing list of responsibilities were the daily chores associated with the feeding and wellbeing of the animals on their family farm, something Sallie used to do. Michael also found himself the sole source for all the families house work, cooking, cleaning, laundry, tending to the boy's school work and activities, as well as seeing to the personal hygienic needs of his wife. It was a tremendous responsibility, seemingly one with no end, but one that he did not question, for the love he held for his wife and children could allow for no other response.

Despite the extraordinary changes that had re-coursed her life, there was one constant in Sallie's life that had not wavered. She never forgot her horse. Escogido was the one thing that tied Sallie to this planet. She had forgotten everyone and everything, but she clearly remembered Esco.

Despite her injuries, or perhaps because of them, Sallie was constantly restless. She continued to struggle to find a reason to get up off the couch. Michael would lend support and encouragement, but as soon as Michael got her to her feet, she would say one clear word: "Esco". Each day Sallie made it obvious that she wanted to return to her horse. Michael knew he couldn't allow it. Sallie could barely stand on her own, let alone stand next to, or handle, a stallion. "No, you can't go to the barn," he would tell her. Instead, he would get her bathed, dressed and fed each morning before going to the barn to tend to the horses. Sallie continued to battle nausea, requiring that Michael give her anti-nausea medicine to control her vomiting. He could no longer go to work because his responsibilities were now at home with his wife. Chayce also had to be fed and needed help with school work. Michael found himself swimming in very deep and turbulent waters. The life he knew before that fateful day of the accident had completely changed. He had become the exclusive care provider for all of Sallie's basic life needs, and realized that without his continued attention, any chance she might have for an improvement in her condition would likely be diminished. There were also the daily needs of being a father, tending to the family's farm, and all their animals. And then there was his job…it's what Michael knew best and one of the things he found passion in. Michael was a police officer dedicated to the people he served. He carried several important assignments within the Police Department, and in his absence; some of those duties would be shifted to other people. That was a troubling thought, as he didn't want to burden his partners with covering his responsibilities. Other duties, some that other people might think less important, might fall to the side, and that was also unacceptable to Michael. For most people, such a combination of stress and responsibility might be overwhelming, but Michael knew he would just have to reach deeper in himself to maintain the strength necessary to safeguard what was most important to him. There was no question; it would just have to be that way

It was several days after her release from the hospital that Michael started noticing an interesting pattern with Sallie and Esco. If Sallie was nauseated, he would get to the barn to feed the horses and all the horses would eat except for Esco. That was not Esco, for Esco had a huge appetite. He usually ate twice as much as the horses who were much bigger than he was. Michael also noticed that on those days Sallie was agitated, confused or irritable, Esco would be rake his teeth up and down the stall bars to his stall door. Michael often found himself trying to console Esco. He would chat with Esco and say, "I know, Esco. I'm sorry buddy. I miss her, too". Other times he had to administer Banamine, a drug used to combat colic in horses, then walk him in the arena for long periods of time. Despite Michael's efforts, Esco developed colic. As Michael continued to treat Esco with the Banamine, he came to realize that he would also have to administer an anti-nausea medication to Sallie. Between Sallie and Esco, Michael was doing the work of four people.

It was a week after she left the hospital that Michael took Sallie for her scheduled follow-up with her regular physician. Their family doctor went through the hospital reports. He said, "Boy, she really rang her bell, didn't she?" Michael asked, "Is there anything more I should be doing for her. Is there anything more I should know?" The doctor simply replied, "She needs all the rest she can get. You are doing a great job with her. Keep up the good work". According to her family doctor, the file sent from the hospital indicated that there was neither facial trauma nor broken bones. She simply had a concussion with a few bleeds and rest and time would tell. Michael asked when Sallie would be normal again, and the doctor compassionately replied, "In time. These things take time." He then gave Sallie a quick examination before sending the couple home. As difficult as the visit was for Michael, trying to understand what was happening to his wife, Sallie was also struggling. Throughout their visit, Sallie kept pointing to the door of the exam room as if demanding to leave. Michael struggled to keep her calm and quiet through the appointment, and the lack of answers, combined with Sallie's insistence to leave, left Michael frustrated and struggling to understand why this was happening to their family.

In the days following their visit to the doctor, Sallie developed an infection requiring antibiotics. The medicine came in the form of black and yellow capsules. Sallie called them "bumblebees" because they made her stomach hurt, and she resisted taking them. Sallie would often tear the capsules apart and look at the powder inside instead of taking them. Watching her, Michael would run out of patience, telling her "Take the damn pill"..

In the meantime, Chayce had finally returned home, having spent the days since the accident with a neighbor. Chayce had learned that Esco had fallen on his mom and that the ambulance had taken his mom to the hospital. Chayce quickly realized that something was different but still didn't understand what was going on with his mom. He tried to talk to her, not realizing how seriously she was hurt. "Mom! Mommy! Mom, it's me! Chayce! Your son," he would say. "Don't you remember me?" But Sallie didn't recognize him. In fact, everyone was a stranger to Sallie. She simply did not respond and couldn't connect any of the dots that now defined her life. After a while, Chayce would walk away, sad and frustrated. "Dad, is mom ever going to be the same?" he would ask. Michael would simply say, "I hope so."

As if a cruel irony, Michael and Sallie had finished a long remodeling of their house only weeks before the accident. While working on the project, they had moved out of the house and into a small travel trailer on their property for several months. Now she found herself feeling lost and disoriented in the house she was told was her home, and this only added to the stress Michael was feeling. In response, Chayce had become a calming counterpoint to his dad's assertive voice. Because Sallie could not remember who she was, or the people around her, Michael had to set strong limits with Sallie. This produced feelings of mistrust in him, as she simply had no idea what was happening around and to her. She started to believe that Michael was trying to poison her with the black and yellow pills used to fight her infection, and no longer had any sense of time or space. The days turned into weeks, and Michael tried to handle it all. There were moments when Michael would bark at Sallie in frustration, and Chayce would appear to see what was happening. And in his own way, Chayce would try to help. Recalling the couple's bantering while they remodeled their home, Chayce would laugh and say, "Dad! You two joked too much about burying each other in the perk holes out back. Remember all last summer when you were building the house? You and mom would get frustrated with each other and you would joke with her, 'Don't think for one minute you won't fit in one of those perk holes, Sallie"! The pills hurt her stomach. She thinks you are trying to kill her." And he would laugh, and so would Michael. And Sallie would just look at them both, wide eyed, not really understanding the significance of the conversation.

Throughout the third week she was home, Sallie slept most of the time. Chayce was learning to take the new circumstances in stride. He would arrive home and wake his mom. Using his calm and easygoing personality, he had started finding ways to help. Determined to have a conversation with her, Chayce began holding objects in front of her and saying their names. "These are your keys, can you say key? K-k-k-e-e-e-y-y-y…" Sallie had a difficult time with making clear sounds. She had a difficult time with pronouncing R's, S's and L's. Chayce's mom was always correcting his speech before. She had always been very capable of conversation and helped him with homework. And he remembered, he, himself had had difficulty forming the same letters when he was young. Chayce searched the Internet for "Speech Therapy" and found tongue exercises used for patients who had had strokes and lost the control of their tongue. He instructed his mother to put her tongue to the roof of her mouth. However she seemed to not understand what the roof of her mouth was, nor did she understand how to move her tongue side to side. Chayce knew the tongue was a muscle and the young athlete that he was, he knew muscles had to be strengthened. He also knew from playing football how hard it was to speak with his mouth guard in. Recognizing that the mouth guard requires a person to work all the muscles in their mouth and face, he convinced his dad to pick up a rubber mouth guard just like the one he had for football. The following day Michael delivered the rubber appliance to Chayce, whereupon he was able to mold the device to fit Sallie's mouth. As the weeks passed, Chayce would wake Sallie up, telling her "Mom, it's time to say your words." He would then place the mouth guard into her mouth. "Mom K-K-K -Keeeeyys, now you say it." With a hunk of rubber in her already crowded mouth, she tried very hard to say the word. He would continue to ask her to repeat words. And she continued to try to repeat the word he asked her to say. Sallie did not realize what Chayce was doing for her, but didn't resist. This just seemed like part of the day and she complied.

One day in particular Chayce pointed to an object in the house asking, "Mom what's that?" Sallie answered, "Fucking Couch." which surprised Chayce. His mom didn't swear. Certainly not in her kids presence! "No, mom it's the 'couch!" He pointed to another object and asked, "Mom what's that?" Sallie answered, "Fucking TV." Again, Chayce was shocked. And said, "NO! MOM! It's the TV! Not the F-word and then TV". He began asking her to name several objects, and each time, she would say "Fucking" before she could say the object. Chayce began to find humor in his mother's swearing. When Michael came home from work that evening, he could not wait to show his dad how much his mom had improved. As Michael came through the door Chayce blurted out, "Dad! Mom can name objects in the house now watch." " Hey mom, what's this?" And Sallie answered, "Fucking remote control". Michael laughed, "Well her speech is clearer. " Michael then asked her what an object was. "Fucking door." Both Michael and Chayce laughed. Michael jokingly said, "Well, good thing we don't have to take her to church." But both were learning this was a new issue that would be one of many to overcome. Sallie had always had good verbal filters. Not anymore!

Chayce became a source of support not only to his mother, but to Michael as well. While Michael would tend to other issues around the farm, Sallie became Chayce's full time after-school job. As days and weeks went on, Sallie's speech started to improve and the swearing would lessen. Some day's it did not appear at all. In a few short weeks of repeatedly practicing numerous words, Sallie showed great progress in her speech.

When four or five weeks had passed, and Sallie was showing some improvement, Michael finally began letting friends know about Sallie's accident. He didn't talk to them about her condition. He fell back to the principles of a good police officer, delivering only the facts about the accident and that she was home, but not engaging in the emotion, nor describing their circumstances at home. Michael believed that Sallie was getting better, and decided people could visit her if they wanted.

Her cousin, Litonya, scolded Michael for not calling her sooner, then got into the car with her mother, Lynne, to make the one hour road trip from Tacoma to the farm to see Sallie. Both were shocked by the changes they saw in Sallie. Usually talkative, Sallie now struggled to find the right words. While Litonya was sure Sallie recognized her, Sallie couldn't say her name. She couldn't remember the name of "that thing that mixes up the clothes." Litonya and Lynne readily knew something was seriously wrong. It seemed Sallie's mind had regressed to that of a 5-year-old. And Michael looked lost.

In the weeks since the accident, Sallie had begun to call her grandfather. A self-made and successful man, he was always the rock in her life while growing up. Now she wanted to converse with him. Each time she would open the call by saying "Hi grandpa!", but it would come out in a child-like voice. Then, like a young nervous child who didn't know what to say, she would hang up. Each time Michael would then get a phone call from grandpa, who would inquire, "Michael, how is Sallie doing?" Michael would respond by telling him, "yeah she had an accident…". Grandpa would interject," Michael, I know she had an accident. You called me from the hospital… Has she been to the doctor yet, any new information? Update? Details, please," he would bluntly demand. Michael would respond, "Yeah, I took her to the doctor. The doctor says it's just going to take time. Grandpa would then retort, " Okay, keep me posted." And that was the extent of the conversation. Grandpa was always short and to the point. In her lifetime Sallie had always known him to be someone who didn't want to hear drama. He just wanted the facts. So that was what Michael gave him, and that's where each call would end.

After about five weeks, Michael felt confident that Sallie could use a walker to get around the house and the handrail to get herself upstairs, if he wasn't there to help her. He moved her back into their bedroom. Her improving condition and awareness brought yet another set of problems, as Sallie was constantly asking Michael to do things, and he was barely able to sleep. Sallie had always been a fiercely independent person, so her persistent neediness, at this point, introduced yet more strain on the family. It would not be uncommon for Sallie to awake at 3 a.m., saying "Cookie. Cookie... please Cookie!" Sallie was endlessly needy, always asking Michael to do something. After a long day of serving the public, Michael now found himself at home each night, exhausted and feeling like he had nothing left to give. None the less, there would be more requests. Sometimes Sallie needed a glass of water, or something to eat, other times she needed to use the bathroom. Michael understood the limitations brought on by her injuries, but dearly missed Sallie's independence. With her constant demands and questions, Sallie was driving Michael crazy.

CHAPTER 2
GLIMMER OF HOPE

Sallie had no clear recollection of the first 6 week's home from the hospital, but her memory would sporadically return in surprising ways. Before the accident, Sallie and Michael had bred a mare, which became overdue during the early weeks of Sallie's recovery. Knowing how much Sallie cared for the mare, Michael set up a foaling monitor and put it next to Sallie. It worked. Michael was able to keep Sallie occupied and in bed, as she watched the foaling monitor constantly. He was still afraid she would try to walk and fall, because she still could not move without assistance, was unsteady on her feet and still seemingly lost when dealing with people who seemed to know her, but whom she did not recognize.

In spite of all her memory lapses and confusion, the night of March 21, 2008 evidenced a flash of the old Sallie. She had been home for six weeks, struggling to remember most anything from her former life, when she recognized that the mare was about to give birth. Suddenly she said to Michael, "Baby is coming!" Michael wasn't sure if Sallie was correct, but decided to take the chance. He bundled her in warm clothes. She was still unable to walk on her own, though she was able to move about some with a walker. He put her in the truck and drove her to the foaling stall where the mare was. He lifted Sallie from the truck and placed her on a bale of hay so she could see what was happening.

The mare was steaming. Michael had never seen a foal delivered, but he knew the mare was having difficulty. So did Sallie. To Michael's astonishment, Sallie began to instruct him on what needed to be done to help the mare! Sallie had been through foaling several times in her past. She had always felt she could actually communicate with her horses. She often spoke with them intuitively and saw their communications back to her in pictures, a phenomenon actually practiced by special people in the horse world. But she hadn't remembered any of this. Sallie recognized the baby was stuck, because it was too big, so Sallie, speaking very clearly for the first time since her accident, told Michel how to reposition the foal's feet, and with each contraction, how to pull the feet down toward the mare' hocks. As the foal slid through the birth canal, Sallie told him to break the amniotic bag the instant the foal was out of the mare, so the baby could breathe. For the first time, Michael assisted in the birth of a foal, and for the first time, he found hope that Sallie might eventually return to her normal self. Her speech at that moment was crystal clear. And they both watched with satisfaction as the mare cleaned the foal, and the foal, after some time, got his little legs underneath himself, and finally tottered to the belly of the mare to nurse. He was a big foal, so it took some time for him to get those long legs under himself to accomplish this feat. In those moments following the birth, Michael experienced double victories. He had helped to bring a living foal into the world, and his wife had spoken with clarity and decisiveness for the first time since her accident. Though Michael thought this success would be momentary in duration, he would soon discover that Sallie would continue to speak more clearly from that point on. Perhaps they were turning a corner.

Following the foal's birth, Sallie continued to spend her days staring out the window, looking at Esco, whispering "Esco come to me." And day after day, she asked to ride him. "No," Michael would tell her in reply. "Babe, you had an accident. You bonked your head. You have a concussion. You can't ride until you're better." However none of this registered with Sallie. She had no idea what a concussion was, or who this person was that was stopping her. She only knew she wanted Esco. She remembered Esco, and he was the one thing that tied her to knowing she belonged on this earth. Night after night, Sallie would ask Michael, "Am I better yet?" "No," Michael would reassure her calmly. "Not yet, but you are getting better."

Sallie would cry herself to sleep while Michael held her tight. He could feel her frustration, and he recognized the yearning she had to touch the stallion. However he also knew her only chance at recovery lay with his resolve to see her heal in the face of her requests. Each night, Sallie went to bed wondering if she'd be better in the morning. And morning after morning, she would awaken bleary-eyed in a spinning room. Her tongue was swollen, and her face would hurt. When she looked in the mirror, she didn't recognize the person peering back at her. She had begun using a walker to get around, though she remained wobbly and not really in control of her body.

It was Easter morning when Sallie awoke to find that she felt like she had returned from a long trip. Michael looked at her and said, "You look better!" Your eyes look more clear." "What do you mean," Sallie asked. Michael just stared at her. Sallie, you look better than you have since your accident." "What accident?" Sallie asked, looking at him in disbelief. Michael then had to explain, as he did often, that she had fallen with the horse, and that she had had a concussion with a couple of bleeds, spent three nights in the hospital and had been recovering for six weeks.

Despite the memory deficits that still existed, the morning represented the first time in months Sallie had a sense of self, felt human, like she belonged in the world. To Sallie it was as though the past few months did not clearly exist. As time would go on, Michael and Chayce would tell Sallie about the challenges she experienced with walking and speaking, but she couldn't relate or remember those periods. That time just didn't exist. It simply felt as though she had returned from a long journey. The room was no longer spinning, and she could now see objects with clarity. Since the birth of the foal, she could also walk without the walker, and, incredibly, had no recollection that she had used one. Sadly, also absent was her memory of the birth of the foal. Sallie discovered that she could now dress herself, and that brought incredible happiness. Though Michael and Chayce were still a mystery to her, other pieces of her mental health were returning. While she still had the thought process of a little child, she spoke like an adult. She still had a limited understanding of what was going on around her in the larger world, but knew when she was in the house, that it was her house. She also knew where the barn was, and resolved to herself that she was going to see her horse. "Michael, I am going to see Esco!" she exclaimed. Michael had to agree. He laughed at her exuberance. "I'll go with you."

He drove her down the hill to the barn and helped her out of the truck. Sallie's hands were clumsy, and she was still wobbly on her feet when she tried to unlatch Esco's stall door, not strong enough, yet, to pull it open. Michael opened it for her. He was cautious at this first visit, knowing that stallions could be nippy or pushy. He stood between the horse and his wife. Sallie could touch Esco, but Michael would stand ready should something unexpected happen.

As Sallie entered the stall, Esco's eyes lit up. He stretched out his massive neck and laid his head gently on Sallie's chest. Sallie eased into the comfort and familiarity of her special horse. She stroked his face. "Esco, I am so sorry I have been broken," she said. "I've missed you. I can't ride you yet." Michael stood at the ready, and at that moment, Esco pinned his ears and nipped at Michael. Sallie was able to pull Esco back toward her. She patted his neck but recognized the familiar exhaustion that followed any effort. This sensation remained a daily menace to Sallie. She whispered, "I will get better, Esco, and you and I will ride again soon." Michael walked Sallie out of the barn. As they passed the mare's stall, Sallie saw the foal and exclaimed, " Wow, he's huge! When did he get here," she asked Michael. Michael laughed. "Sallie, you're funny. You were there." Sallie had no idea what he was talking about. Had she seen the mare's delivery without remembering it? It was something she'd have to think about later—right now, she felt exhausted, and her sight was foggy.

April would become a good month for Sallie. She had begun to understand how time worked. She knew what a day was, and that if she went to sleep on Monday night, the next morning would be Tuesday. She remembered her grandparents, whom she loved and adored. Her grandmother was always the person Sallie had called when something was going on in her life. If Sallie did well at something, her grandmother would be happy for her. And if Sallie was going through something difficult, she could count on her grandmother to simply listen and offer compassion and understanding, never advice or judgment.

Sallie's ability to converse was also improving, and one morning day that April she called her grandmother.

"Well, hello, you sound so much better," Sallie's grandmother said.

Sallie had no idea what Grandma was talking about, but thought maybe she'd had a cold the last time they spoke.

"I am really good, Grandma. I miss riding Esco though."

In that moment the line went momentarily silent. "You're not getting back on him, are you?" Grandma finally replied.

"Yes," Sallie said, confused. "I can't wait to ride Esco. I miss him and he misses me."

"Are we talking about the same horse?"

"Grandma, it's my horse, Esco," Sallie said, growing frustrated. "That is who I am talking about. I only have one."

Grandma's voice was quiet. "How's your forehead, hon?" she asked Sallie.

Puzzled, Sallie put the phone down and touched her head. Then she picked up the phone and said, "It's fine, my head is fine. My bump is getting better, I think. Anyway, Michael is being mean. He says I can't ride Esco yet." Actually, Michael still refused to let her get off the porch by herself. "He's just worried about you, hon," her grandmother said. "If he is telling you no, I would listen. You married one heck of a guy there."

"No, he is not nice! He won't let me ride Esco!"

"He will in time," Grandma said.

"Yeah, I'm young, so there is time," Sallie said.

Grandma laughed. "Life goes by fast, Sallie." Sallie didn't know what she was talking about. Her days seemed like an eternity to get through.

"Not mine, Grandma. Mine is going by slow."

"Well, babe, take it slow, trust me. Sometimes it seems just like yesterday I was 37."

Sallie was getting frustrated. "Grandma, I am 37, not 72! That is a long time away. That is old."

"Well, it may seem like a long time away, but it can go by quick."

"All right Grandma, I will take it slow," Sallie said. The conversation was making her tired, and she could tell her speech was slurred. "I need to go and sleep."

"Have a good nap, sweetheart."

After Sallie hung up the phone, she fell asleep almost instantly, and when she woke up, she felt as if a long time had gone by. She sat up very quickly and became very dizzy. Her head felt sloshy, as if it had an ocean of water in it. She had a sudden urge to run to the mirror to see if she was 72, but her dizziness stopped her.

Once she had regained her balance and her eyes could focus, Sallie called Michael who was at work.

"Am I 72?" she demanded.

Michael laughed. "No, you are 37."

"Don't laugh. There's not much difference between 37 and 72." Sallie could hear noises from Michael's end of the phone.

He laughed again. "Oh, OK. As much as I would love to argue about this with you, I am working a case and have to go. See you tonight when I get home ."

Sallie's vision had begun to clear. In her mind, seeing more clearly, being able to walk all by herself, dress herself, shower all by herself, meant that she was better. She was determined to ride Esco and decided she had had enough of Michael telling her no. She knew she was better.

It was a few days later when Sallie met Michael at the door. "Where are you going?" Michael asked as she approached the front door. Sallie kept walking. "I am going to ride Esco, and I don't care what you say."

"You stop at that door and come here," Michael said.

Sallie turned and walked into the living room to face Michael. She saw daggers in his eyes.

"Yes," she said in a short tone.

"Sallie, Esco fell on you. You are better, but you're not quite ready yet."

Sallie stamped her foot. "Yes, I am!" she shouted. "I am better! And I feel better when I get to pet him even!"

Michael looked as if he had just been shocked by the electric fence. "You had better not be petting him when I'm not home," he warned her. Sallie glared at him. "I do pet him when you're not home," she said. "He is my friend! He likes me, and he does not say no!" She started to cry. Michael took a deep breath. "You can't even drive yet," he said patiently. "How are you going to ride?" Drive! Sallie thought. Her tears stopped. She remembered driving. She used to drive all the time and go many places. "I want to drive," she said, starting to cry again. "It's not time yet. Pretty soon you can drive, but not yet. You are not better yet." It was apparent that neither Sallie, nor Michael, would yield to the other in that moment, so that was where the discussion ended.

The next day, while Michael was at work and Chayce was at school, Sallie noticed their truck and Drive! popped into her head. Her neck was hurting, and she decided to go to the chiropractor. It was only a short distance from her home. For some reason, she fully remembered the chiropractor quite well. She found a set of keys. That was it—she was going to drive herself to the chiropractor.

She was very nervous getting into the truck, and the engine was much louder than she remembered. As she sat in the truck's cab, other memories came back—she knew how to put the truck in reverse to back it up and put it in drive to go forward. She knew where the gas and brake pedals were. She then pulled out of the driveway and onto the road.

She was very nervous, especially when familiar objects like trees and houses loomed. Another car appeared suddenly on the side of the road. The driver seemed nice, taking a moment to wave at Sallie. A little farther along, she passed another car on the side of the road, and that driver waved at Sallie as well. As she approached the chiropractor's office, a third driver shouted to her.

Sallie parked the truck. She could feel herself getting tired, and knew she had to hurry before she got really sleepy. The doctor seemed surprised to see her and asked what she had been doing to make her neck hurt. "Nothing, being lazy," Sallie said.

"Have you been riding?" he asked.

"No, and Michael won't let me."

"Michael won't let you, huh?" the doctor said. "When did that happen, Michael not letting you?"

Sallie brightened. Clearly her chiropractor was on her side. "Michael said I can't ride since Esco fell on me, but I don't think Michael likes Esco. Esco did not fall. I would remember it if that happened."

"Did you go to St. Pete's?"

"Michael says that I did." She replied.

He left the room for a few minutes. When he returned, he said, "Well, you definitely have a reason for your neck to hurt. Let's fix it." He adjusted Sallie's neck, explaining that certain disks were dislocated based on her recent CT scan findings. Sallie did not understand what he was talking about, but she noticed that after the adjustment, she no longer felt dizzy and her neck felt better. "Tell Michael hello, and come back if you need me," her doctor said. Driving home was not nearly as nerve-racking as the trip there. Sallie saw no other cars at all. She arrived home very tired and settled down for a long nap.

Michael had been home from work for a while when Sallie woke up. She couldn't wait to tell him that she went to the chiropractor by herself. "I can drive!" she said proudly. "I can drive and people were happy to see me. Even the cars on the side of the road waved to me!" Michael stood silent and unsmiling. It was with a feeling of disbelief he replied, "You what?"

"The doc said to tell you hello," Sallie told him.

Michael took a breath of deep frustration. "You," he said. "You need to just go to bed. Go! You go right now." Sallie tried to tell him she had just woken up, but he was too frustrated to listen. "Go!" he told her, and with that she retreated back to the security of her bed.

Sallie was up very early the next day. She chatted with Michael while he was getting ready for work, asking him again if she was 72. "No, you are only 37," he said. "And what are you doing up so early?"

"I slept all day yesterday. I was really tired after driving home."

Michael shook his head. "You do not drive today. You're not ready yet."

But in Sallie's mind, she was hearing her grandmother's voice: "It seems like I was just 37 yesterday."

"When will I be better?" Sallie asked. "I am 37, and tomorrow I am going to be 72, and I still wouldn't have ridden Esco yet." She started to cry.

Michael calmed her down. "You won't be 72 tomorrow, and you are getting better. On my next set of days off I will teach you to drive. OK?" Sallie hugged him for the first time since the accident. It was an impulsive reaction. He was going to teach her to drive. She knew this was her gateway to ride. She still didn't remember how he fit in her life, but he was her guard and guide to being able to ride Esco! He lightly wiped the tears from her cheek. "You are getting better every day."

Sallie followed him down the stairs and into the kitchen. After he got his coffee, Sallie followed him out the door and waved to him as he got into his car. "No petting Esco, and no driving!" Michael called to her. Sallie just smiled and waved. Michael gave her a stern look, pointed his finger at Sallie, and said, "Don't you get off the porch. I mean it. If I come home from work, and you got off the porch, I will know that you got off the porch, and you are going to be in BIG Trouble! You do NOT get off that porch!" Something in his tone told Sallie he was serious. She did not get off the porch that day, not even to pet Esco. In fact, Sallie would not get off the porch alone for a very long time.

Over the next three months, Sallie really started to like Chayce, in spite of his still being a stranger to her. She liked that he was smart, and he could draw. In her childlike mind, she learned that he had paperwork to do every day after school. Sallie didn't like his paperwork, but he said he had to do it, or he would get in trouble. Sallie didn't want him to get into trouble—she was in trouble all the time, it seemed, and it did not feel good. So he had given her something to read to keep her busy. She would later understand that he had been giving her his sixth grade weekly reader, a childhood publication meant for children in the sixth grade.

So, while Chayce did his work at the kitchen table, Sallie would color, or look at the pictures in the weekly reader. Sometimes he'd ask for her help, and she'd try to help him, but she did not know all the answers.

Chayce had books. Sallie remembered that she used to read books— lots of books. But when she looked at Chayce's books, the words didn't look like words. The letters looked like little pictures. Quickly, Chayce realized his mother could not read. Every day when he got home, he would do his homework and give Sallie a book to read. He started showing her the letters, written out one by one, A, B, C, until she thought they looked like letters again. Soon, she was able to see letters and sound out some words. She began reading a few sentences, and then paragraphs. She could say all the words. "Tell me what you just read about," Chayce would ask. "Words," Sallie replied. He would laugh at that. "Funny, Mom. What was the story about?" Sallie did not know. To her, there was no story, just words.

Sallie didn't know it at the time, but two of Chayce's teachers were helping both of them. As they did Chayce's homework together, Chayce's grades went downhill fast. Sixth grade was the only year he brought home C's and D's and one F. He was still learning about math, and every day he would check his homework answers with his sixth-grade teacher. Chayce told the teacher what was going on, and it seemed that the teacher understood the situation better than Chayce did. With the teacher's help, Chayce was able to raise his grades to A's and B's by the end of that year— and teach his mom the skills he was learning. He was a student at school and a teacher at home.

Chayce was not a moody child, just preoccupied. On one occasion his sixth-grade teacher asked him how he was doing. He didn't tell her about his mother's accident or her need to relearn basic skills, but she could see that something was wrong. The only thing on his mind while he was in school was how to delay going home. He didn't like all the tasks he was asked to do: vacuuming, sweeping, mopping, dishes, and moving hay. For a while, Sallie couldn't move well, and with Michael back to work, that meant Chayce had been taking over more household chores than before. Sometimes he was on guard duty and had to make sure Sallie didn't go anywhere while Michael had to work on weekends or late weeknights. Chayce would stay up and wait for his dad. It was a big responsibility for an 12-year-old.

Michael's days off finally arrived, the days when he would finally teach an eager Sallie how to drive their truck. Michael didn't seem happy as he reminded her to take her purse with her driver's license. The reality of putting Sallie behind the wheel of the truck was a concern for him. He took a deep breath and sighed, as she took her time getting to the truck. "Stop breathing," Sallie told him. "I'm going as fast as I can. If you don't like it, just stop breathing." He laughed. "Just stop breathing, huh? I bet sometimes you'd wish I would just stop breathing." Sallie smiled. It was true, she didn't like his deep sighing, as it usually meant she was in trouble. He sighed a bit more as he asked her to put the truck in reverse and back out slowly.

"I said slowly!"

Startled, Sallie slammed on the brakes, jarring them both.

"Good, now put the truck in drive and go forward slowly—I said slowly!"

Sallie hit the brakes again, and they both pitched forward.

"Put the truck in park," Michael said sharply.

When she had done so, he continued, "Hands on the steering wheel at 10 o'clock and two o'clock. I want to see both hands on the wheel, and do not move them or take them off the steering wheel, do you understand? When you place your foot on the gas pedal, you softly press down on the pedal. When you need to stop, you put your foot on the brake and you softly press down on the brake. None of this stomping crap."

Sallie nodded, put the truck into drive, and eased it down the driveway.

"Let's take a right," Michael said, and Sallie looked for cars coming from both directions.

"Blinkers! Turn your blinker on. There will be no shortcut crap driving here. No, the other blinker! And keep both hands on the wheel, 10 o'clock and two o'clock."

Every time Michael took a deep breath, Sallie got nervous.

"I said 10 o'clock and two o'clock," he reminded her. "Stay in your own lane. Sallie, stay in this lane…this lane."

Michael grabbed the steering wheel. "This side of the yellow line."

"I do not like this driving lesson!" Sallie said.

"Don't worry, I don't like it either", he mused.

Sallie drove a few miles, making a loop so that soon she returned home.

"I thought I would never be so happy to see my own driveway," she said.

"Good, that makes two of us."

Sallie turned into the driveway, pulled up to the house, and parked the truck.

"Yay!" she yelled. "I can ride Esco now!"

Michael shook his head. "Not yet. You're not ready yet."

Told "no" yet again, Sallie sat still while silent tears streamed down her face. In this moment, she truly felt imprisoned. She had been told that she had an accident, of which she still had no memory There was little explanation of what happened that she could understand or remember. "So what if she had an accident. she thought. It's over. I am here. I want my life back" She knew she was tired a lot, but desperately wanted back her life as she remembered it. At this point, some four months after the accident, she remembered she had grandparents, she worked, she drove and she rode Esco. For Sallie, that was all she knew.

"I need a nap," she said. "When I wake up I am going to go pet Esco."

She expected Michael to say no to petting Esco, but he said nothing. Later that day, Sallie went to the barn by herself. She spent her time petting Esco, and much to her surprise, discovered that she was not in trouble with Michael.

In the days that followed, Michael gave her several more driving lessons. After every lesson, Sallie would be very tired and need to nap for hours. But with each drive, she was getting better and better at staying in her own lane and keeping both hands on the wheel. She tried not to get yelled at. If she did not get yelled at, it meant she did a good job.

As the days and weeks passed, Chayce continued to be more and more fun to be around and was becoming Sallie's favorite person. They still worked together at the kitchen table every night, Chayce, finishing his homework, and Sallie, reading pages of words. One night, Sallie read the words faster than she did before. She switched to coloring until Chayce finished his work and asked, "Mom, what was the story about?" Sallie continued coloring her picture. "It was about a dog. He got lost and had to find his home again." "Mom, that's right!" Chayce said. "You read your first story."

At that moment, Sallie suddenly remembered that she worked. She had a job and clients. She had a boss. She grabbed the phone and called her boss. "Larry, this is Sallie. I have clients," she said. "Yes you do. Are you ready to come back to work?" "Yes!" Larry said, "OK, kiddo, well, I have news first." Your license expired on your birthday. You need to get your clock hours to renew your license." Sallie remembered clock hours—the 60 hours of continuing education required per year to keep a real estate agent's license active.

CHAPTER 3
JUMPING THROUGH HOOPS!

"Chayce," Sallie said. "I have to work on the computer. I need to get my clock hours in." Chayce knew exactly what that meant and knew where to look for the phone number she needed. Within a few days, Sallie was reading short paragraphs, answering questions, and taking quizzes. She struggled with the content at first, but after several weeks of daily work, she finally completed her clock hours in June. As before, Sallie's memory and skill would suddenly come to her in chunks.

It was during June, that Sallie went to sign up her first listing. Michael went with her for support, as she was extremely nervous about meeting new people, about testing her re-acquired skills and about driving. Though she would continue to be a nervous wreck, she had begun doing real estate deals as long as someone co-listed with her and checked her work. Her ability to process information was impaired, and she still needed help filling in purchase and sales agreements, but it was a start.

Sallie was progressing. Michael agreed to let her drive to the gas station, or the chiropractor, as long as she would come right home. Once she had completed her clock hours and was able to drive short distances,

Sallie believed she had to be doing much better. However, she hesitated to ask Michael's opinion. Every time she overcame a challenge and thought she was better, it was still not enough for Michael to agree to let her ride Esco.

While the initial months following her accident were a blur, June continued to bring clarity. Sallie spent more time in the barn brushing Esco. Michael gave her a lesson on how to clean the horse's hooves with the hoof pick. As they groomed Esco, Michael said, "I want you to go to the doctor and ask if it is OK for you to ride Esco."
Sallie looked at him.
"I think you're ready now," he said. "I'll go with you, and you will drive there." While Michael had not come to this decision easily, he recognized the efforts Sallie had made toward recovery. He knew he had set expectations for her that, while not easily attained, represented the best interests for a safe recovery. She met each challenge he set out for her, and it would be up to the doctor to decide if she was physically ready. Sallie made the appointment, hardly daring to hope that the doctor would agree to let her ride. On the day of the appointment, Sallie drove to the doctor's office with Michael. He did not comment on her driving, so Sallie thought she must have done a good job.

The doctor met them with a smile. "Hi, Sallie, you look like you're doing great. How are things?" Sallie wasn't sure she was doing great—she still wasn't allowed to do so many things that she used to do, but she decided to tell the doctor her accomplishments. "Fine, I guess. I finished my clock hours. It took much longer than it ever did before, but I did finish them. And I drove here. So I think I am doing good." Sallie paused to gather her courage. "What I really want to know is, can I ride Esco?" The doctor looked over her chart and gave Sallie a quick examination. "How is her balance?" he asked Michael.

"Much better" he replied.

"How is the vertigo?" he asked Sallie.

"Not as bad as it was."

"OK," the doctor said, "you want to know if you can ride your horse. Is this Esco? Is that the name I am reading on your chart?"

Sallie smiled. "Yes, that's him."

"I don't see why you can't get on him—but you have to wear a helmet, Sallie," the doctor said seriously. "You really rang your bell. You had a good concussion. I want you to have a helmet on." What the doctor was unaware of was the complexity of injuries Sallie had sustained that Februrary day. He had no information or records describing the bone fractures or jaw damage she sustained, nor the nerve damage or other complications that continued to seriously impede any lasting progress, and of which Sallie and Michael were still unaware. Instead He was responding to what he read about and to his observations of her from this and her previous visits.

Sallie couldn't believe what she had just heard. "I can? I really can? I can ride Esco?" "Yes, you really can, but with a helmet on. And Michael, you will be there to make sure, right?" Michael answered, "Yeah, she's not riding by herself ever again." "Good call. And Sallie, enjoy your ride on Esco."

But she was not to ride Esco just yet, Michael told her on the drive home. "Esco has had a lot of time off," he said. Though Sallie arranged for Esco to be worked by a woman she had hired while she was healing, Michael was still erring on the side of caution. "I want you to ride Cody first."

Sallie had to agree with Michael. She doubted her own abilities as she had begun to recognize some of the issues she was struggling with. Michael had ridden Esco a couple of times when Sallie had first started Esco's training four months prior to the accident. So he felt confident he could bring Esco back to work by riding him on his days off. But each and every ride Michael had had on Esco was a fight. Esco seemed to be resentful and defiant with Michael, who though not a professional, was a good rider in his own right. After a few rides, Michael clearly saw Esco was over his own head and agreed Esco needed a professional rider to put two months of rides on him and bring him back to work.

She reached out to friends who knew Esco, and asked if they knew of someone who could ride him, as she had had an accident.

To Sallie's shock, her friends already knew about the accident. How did they know?

"Sallie, you called." they told her.

"I what? I called? When?" she replied.

"Oh, you called from the hospital. You were really out of it."

She would be silent and respond with a "giggle". But, internally, she really started to struggle with what she knew, and what she did not know. This would begin to set a new pattern in her life, a pattern of second guessing herself and everything around her.

It was not an easy task to find someone who would ride a stallion who fell while under saddle, but eventually, a rider agreed to work with Esco for the next month. At the same time, Sallie would ride Cody. Cody was a sweetheart, a gentle giant. Half Andalusian and half Tennessee walking horse, Cody was a beautiful black horse that Michael and Sallie had raised since he was a 7-month-old colt. Michael wanted Sallie to get the feel of riding again. For Sallie, the first rides on Cody were nothing much, just saddling him up, getting on, and walking. She felt no joy in walking around the arena on Cody, but knew this was the only way she'd be able to ride

Esco.

Happily for Sallie, Michael thought she did fine, despite a few wobbles in her balance and intermittent bouts of vertigo. Esco had always been very gentle with Sallie, but not so much with Michael. On the ground, Esco treated Michael like a buddy, reaching out with his nose and tickling Michael's cheek. He would be a sweetheart until Michael would get on him. Then the fight was on. Esco would buck or rear, or he'd puff up, thrusting his chest so far out that his front feet barely touched the ground. Michael would have to be a strong disciplinarian to get Esco to do what he asked. He'd get irritated with the stallion that was gentle with Sallie, but a fighter with him. It was simply part of working with Esco; Esco was moody. The day Sallie was to ride, Michael stood observing as the trainer dismounted Esco. The trainer, who had been working with Esco, was happy to turn him over to Sallie. She had personally hated the horse and found him to be very difficult! OK, he's not doing anything. He'll be OK, Michael thought.

At last, it was Sallie's turn, and she and Esco were both ready. "Esco, it has been a long time, son," Sallie told him. "I promise to be good to your mouth and to you. Please be good for me." Esco looked her in the eye, and then gently nuzzled Sallie's trembling hands. She spoke to him the entire time as she mounted. He was very attentive, tilting one ear back toward Sallie and listening for every cue. He began licking and chewing, which meant he was relaxed, happy, and willing. They walked off from the mounting block as though nothing had ever happened. During the ride, Sallie felt as though she was home. Sitting on Esco was her favorite place on this earth to be. With each stride Esco took, her head felt clearer. The sounds of Esco's wet moist mouth playing with the bit, were comforting to her. Hearing his hooves in the sand was a sound she had longed for. Feeling the warmth of 1200 lbs under her gave her soul a familiar freedom that she remembered from what seemed so long ago. While trying to maintain her balance on Esco, she remembered her very first ride on a horse. She was 3 years old. She felt safe and free. Sallie gently extended her hand down to pat Esco's neck. It was a struggle for her, as her balance and coordination were not back by any means. Michael observed Sallie was just starting to slip too far to one side in the saddle. She looked physically uncoordinated and weaker, unlike the strong confident rider she had been when she started the young, tenacious stallion. Before he could say a word, Sallie felt the whole arena begin to spin. The sky, the trees and the white sand suddenly blurred. Michael had not even had a chance to move when Esco came to a halt, turned his neck and head back to look at Sallie. She caught herself, leaning forward to rest on his neck, while he lifted his head up to meet her. The pair then sat silently, waiting out the vertigo that had overtaken her head. "He loves you, babe. His eye is very soft. I'm not sure I've ever seen a horse love a human as much as he loves you." As he walked up to hold Esco and help Sallie dismount, Esco once again began to muzzle Sallie's leg. Michael helped her down from the saddle, and Esco muzzled and tousled her hair. He seemed to be checking nearly every inch of her body, from head to toe, with his muzzle, making certain she was alright. As he was doing so, Sallie said "Esco, I'm sorry. I am so sorry I got hurt and was not here." Esc nickered softly, nearly a whisper, as if to say, "…me too, I missed you too!" All three walked back to the barn to feed Esco and put him up for the night.

After 6 long hard months, Sallie and Esco were finally back together. With each and every ride over the next two months, Sallie remembered more and more of her life and the people in it. By July, Sallie's phone was ringing steadily with real estate clients. She had no idea why they wanted to use her. It made no sense to her at all. She felt so awkward, so out of place. But each client seemed to have faith in her abilities. She often said, "I had a concussion with a couple of bleeds, I can refer you to someone." But they were confident she was who they wanted to use. Sallie's peers were aware she had this injury as well. One thing Sallie had always been was ethical. She had a strong sense of justice woven into her being. She was very concerned she might make a poor decision for any one. And she expressed this to her brokers. To her surprise, they were supportive and compassionate and agreed to check her work.

This insecurity came from the fact that despite several months passing since her fall, she still did not know Chayce or Michael. However, she did know Escogido. Knowing Esco and riding him again was familiar. It gave her some faith that she might know real estate, another piece of the puzzle of her life. Everyone seemed to think she knew the real estate market. Though everyone on the outside of the house kept telling her what a great husband Michael was, and how great her two sons Rian and Chayce were, she struggled to remember. She still wasn't able to recognize with understanding the sacrifices they had made and were making to care for her. She was still struggling to place them and to feel the connections. She was coming to understand she had kids, but who they were was still very much an unknown, a deep, internal, silent and very private struggle. Her son Chayce knew, and Michael knew, she could not place them in her life. But they all kept that to themselves. Sallie always used to say, "What happens on the farm stays on the farm." In a sense, they were all living that, somehow, subconsciously.

As Sallie was regaining bits and pieces of her sense of who she was and recalling her role in business, Rian, her eldest showed up at her door. He hadn't seen Sallie since the accident, and Sallie hadn't any idea what she knew as she tried to remember who he was. He had come, Sallie was aware, from college to visit. It was a beautiful sunny day, so they had moved to the covered porch enjoying the quiet. The farm spread out below them, grasses glistening in the sunlight, horses moving about the paddocks, nibbling what was left of their hay. It was the first time Sallie had seen Rian, and he had no idea Sallie didn't remember him. (There it was, Michael the stoic policeman, communicating only on a "need to know.") She broke the familiar, yet awkward, silence with a question. "So was I the mother that always beat you two?" "… because it feels like I must have beat you all the time." Both boys laughed in shocked surprise. Rian retorted, "Oh, yeah mom! I remember one whole spanking, so yeah, you beat me all the time. "And he laughed again, peering at her in amazement. Then Chayce popped off, "Yeah mom, I remember three whole spankings, so you beat me all the time! Rian was always your favorite. Rian shot Chayce a condescending glare. "Oh, shut up Chayce. You're such a drama queen. "Why does it feel like I beat you all the time," she asked them. Rian replied, "I don't know mom. You threatened to beat us a lot, but you didn't. But when you said to do something, we just knew to do it!" Sallie dropped her eyes and quipped, "Just checking. I had to be sure I wasn't the mother who destroyed your lives or anything." Rian replied, "Well I'm in college and doing well, so you didn't destroy my life." Chayce shot back, "Well you almost destroyed mine, he cried in his self-righteous 12 year old voice. Rian laughed and rolled his eyes, big brother that he was, and said, "Oh shut up, Chayce." Chayce exclaimed, "She did almost destroy my life. I remember, when all I really wanted to do was kill you. She would make us sit in time out and make us hold hands!" "Oh, I remember, that!" Rian declared as he laughed. "Every time we fought she would make us sit and hold hands in time out." Sallie laughed nervously, and asked, "You would just stay there and sit holding hands? Why would you just stay there and do that?" And they, in unison, spouted back, "Because you looked at us, with that big line across your forehead, and commanded that the first one who broke hands would get their butt spanked, and we believed you!" This conversation helped comfort her about her relationship with her boys and paved the way to reconnect that they were truly her sons.

Sallie was trying hard to make connections with her life, and her memories were clearer at this point with business. So she would take the clients. But before she would give clients a value on their home, she would ask Michael to check her market analysis. When he would say, "Looks correct to me." Sallie, would then ask Chayce to check her work. Chayce would read through her numbers and market analysis. "Looks good Mom. Looks just like your work before." Then...she would hand her market analysis to her broker, "Larry, before I list this, I just want to make sure I absolutely did my work and got my numbers correct." Larry would say, "Looks good kid. Looks real good." Then Sallie could go confidently back to her clients, letting them know the value. Sallie took a few listings. Each one gave her a bit more confidence in her abilities. But, all of her work had to be checked. First by Michael, then Chayce and then her broker Larry. And she refused to give a value if any one of the three had not checked her work. Each client she met with made her very nervous. Clients wanted to know what their properties were worth, and then they wanted to list them with her. She was so concerned with her abilities, she would list properties with other agents as a "co' listing. This gave her back up and a fourth set of eyes to check her work. She never believed in not paying anyone for any service, so it was easy to co-list her listings with agents and split the commission with them. She felt deeply insecure about her work, and at the same time, she was feeling pressure to perform, to make an income, to contribute like she was told she had before.

With each successful closing, her confidence was coming back. She did have that Real Estate Market mastered. It was from all the years prior she spent as a commercial and residential lender. Her connection with Esco had triggered parts of the brain that had seemed to have disappeared. She had a good sense of the market and many thought clearer than most people.

And with each ride she was having on Escogido, she was starting to remember more and more about the market. One day, while riding him, the sun was out, but the wind was blowing. It was a bit turbulent weather-wise. Her mind opened up, and she remembered all the clients she had called, shortly before the accident, letting them know she thought the market was crashing. She recalled that she had advised each client to withdraw offers, as these were investment properties, and she knew these clients did not have the financial staying power to ride out a crash. She was very honest in her business dealings. She realized how she had respected people and their money. She knew how hard people worked for it. Even knowing what she did know of the market, she could have never foreseen just how deep that crash in the market would be. So her business sense became more and more clear, and her clients, more frequent.

Sallie had always intended that she and Esco would compete in dressage. She was feeling more comfortable that she could take care of herself, and drive. She had accomplished all of her clock hours in real estate, managed, even, to successfully close a couple of real estate transactions and to sell a few breeding's from Esco. She had some cash availability for riding lessons. She could ride and no longer experienced vertigo on every ride. It was time for a trainer. Sallie had heard of a trainer who was very good and who served as a judge in dressage competitions. She called and left a message for him. His name was Mike Osinski. It was the end of August of 2008.

CHAPTER 4
MEETING OSINSKI

In the world of dressage, Mike Osinski was known as a successful rider in competitions hosted by an international Equestrian Sports organization, and as a highly ranked judge in the United States. He was also allowed to judge international competitions. He was the recipient of competitive bronze, silver, and gold medals, and a number of his horses had been honored with the title "Horse of the Year" multiple times.

Sallie got a hint of how important Osinski would become to her the moment she heard his calm, comforting voice on the phone. When she told him about Esco and their accident, he responded in a voice that soothed her, just like music did. "I'm glad you can still ride," he said. "But are you OK?" She told him that she'd had a concussion with a couple of bleeds, but that she had recovered and her doctor had released her to ride Esco. "So, I've been riding him at home," Sallie said. "And now I need a trainer to help me with him. I don't want to just ride circles in the back yard forever." "That is what dressage is, circles," Osinski said. "But I do understand what you're saying." He invited her to a local horse show. "Come down and take a look and see if this works for you."

Finally, in September, seven months after the accident, the first day of her first lesson had arrived! Michael hooked the horse trailer to the truck, while Sallie haltered Esco and brushed him. "Esco, we get to go on an adventure!" she told him. "We get to meet our teacher, who is going to help me ride you better." She brushed his glossy coat. "Esco, you have to let me know if you like him. I don't want to hurt you in any way. "Esco looked Sallie in the eye, then lowered his head and began licking and chewing. She knew he understood. She led Esco to the trailer, and he jumped right in.

Michael helped Sallie tie the lead rope through the ring in the horse trailer, as she still did not have full control of her hands. Esco didn't like Michael in the trailer. It was easy to tell, as Esco swung his head violently and pinned his ears back against his head. Michael had to leave the trailer and tie the rope by leaning in through the window. Then they both jumped in the truck. Michael went too, as he didn't think Sallie was ready to haul a horse trailer. "How much will the lesson cost?" Michael asked her. When she told him $75.00 plus the haul in fee, Michael let out a deep heavy sigh. Sallie knew he was unhappy about the expense. But she wasn't going to let his sighing put a damper on her happiness.

As Michael made the turn into the training facility, he asked, "Are we in the right place?" It looked like they had entered a residential community. They drove past 60 acres of paddocks surrounded by pristine white fencing, a barn topped with cupolas, and a 100-by-200-foot enclosed arena, also with cupolas. Michael was impressed with the flawless lawn and the gardens in full bloom. Michael asked "What kind of place is this?" As he drove around the end of the barn, Michael found himself in awe as he had never experienced a professional horse facility like this. It was Sallie who had been to many horse farms. Michael rode for pleasure. Both loved horses and rode for the same reasons, but in different ways. While Sallie had always taken lessons throughout her life, Michael had discovered his sacred place on horseback though his experiences in the mountains.

When Sallie led her horse into the open end of the arena, she felt like she was walking into a coliseum. The arena was huge and incredibly beautiful. At about 200 feet away, Sallie could just make out a gate and a tall, trim man standing next to it, waving.

Esco pushed forward on the lead line and pranced his walk. He wanted to see who that was. As they moved closer, the horse quickened his pace, nearly trotting to meet Sallie's new instructor.

"You must be Sallie," Osinski said, extending his hand. Then, turning to the horse, he said, "and you must be Esco". While the Osinski and Michael introduced themselves, Sallie longed Esco, essentially letting him moved through is gaits at the end of a long line, to get him used to the new place. He pranced and gawked, taking in the new environment. When Esco had settled down, she brought him back to her new coach. "OK, get on and let's see what you've got," Osinski said. Sallie walked up the mounting block, tapping each toe to knock the dirt and sand off the bottom of her boots. Esco wasn't feeling patient with her, though, and was acting like the green, four-year-old stallion that he was. "Would you like me to hold him for you?" Osinski asked. Even with his help, Sallie was clumsy as she got on Esco. She got one foot in the stirrup and quickly and ungracefully threw her leg over Esco's back. Esco immediately wanted to start walking.

Osinski gave his first instructions. "Make a 20-meter circle around me. Just stay right here, and walk him around me. Just let him relax. Give him some pats with your hand to say, 'Good Esco, thank you for being so brave.' " Sallie rode him in the walk and patted him, Esco exhaled. He began licking and chewing. After a few moments in the walk, Osinski asked Sallie to make the reins shorter and pick up the trot. He observed as she walked and trotted Esco, asking questions. They continued in this framework for the first lesson. Mike Osinski was focused on getting acquainted with Esco and Sallie. As they finished, it was decided that the next month of lessons were scheduled to happen every Tuesday.

After Esco was untacked and loaded back in the trailer, Michael had Sallie drive the horse trailer home. The drive for Sallie was just on the edge of being too far. However, she proved she could make the drive, and Michael agreed it was a safe drive and attainable distance. As usual, Sallie had just enough energy to put Esco safely in his stall before trundling up the hill to the house for a long nap.

Several Tuesdays had come and gone, and yet another was about to take place. Sallie felt like an uncoordinated mess, and she was. Riding on Esco, who was more in the mood to look and gawk than get down to business, was not helping her any either. He soon started displaying his "stallionish" side: fierce, stubborn, grumpy, and strong-willed. On one prior occasion, Osinski immediately saw that Esco was too wild for Sallie to handle. It was a dangerous situation, and he didn't want Sallie to get hurt.

He had asked Sallie to "halt," Esco. When she had done so, Osinski walked up to them, patted Esco's neck, then began to address Sallie's leg position. As the coach touched Sallie's leg, Esco had let out a grumbling neigh and struck the ground with his front leg. "Hey, hold him," Osinski said. "Do not allow your horse to do that." But when he reached for Sallie's leg again, Esco repeated the behavior. That was enough for Osinski. "You get off, Sallie. I'll be right back." As he left the arena, Sallie started to worry. "Now you did it, Esco. We're going to be fired!" To her surprise, Osinski returned to the arena, having put on tall boots and a helmet. Sallie handed him Esco's reins.

"Now, Osinski, he can—"

"I know him, Sallie," Osinski said. "I've seen enough of him to know what he is."

He indicated that Esco was to walk up and stand at the mounting block, and she moved him forward into position. Osinski was confident as he patted Esco's neck and hindquarters, simply letting Esco know it was OK to be touched. The horse appeared to become calm, so Osinski stepped up on the stirrup, holding the reins in one hand. He was barely in the saddle when Esco decided to put up a fight—and reared. Osinski was ready, though, and reached for Esco's throat latch, the area immediately beneath his head on the front side of his neck, directing Esco to put his front feet on the ground. Esco obeyed and put his front feet down, but then started bucking. He threw his hind feet high, nearly at the height of Osinski's head. The coach put a stop to that. Esco's behavior was unacceptable, and Osinski needed him to put his hind feet on the ground. Esco did—and reared again. This struggle went on for several minutes, to Sallie's embarrassment—Esco was being as rebellious as they come. To Sallie, it was like watching two boxers in the last round. He was explosive and mad! The whites of Esco's eyes were red and shown white all around. His nostrils flared red and steamed as he snorted deeply his fury. As his feet hit the sand with each explosion, the sand flew. There were several other riders in the arena who watched Esco's tantrum, and because Esco was a Stallion, and stallions are notoriously unpredictable they, nervous for their safety, had taken their horses and run for cover! But, as mortified as she was, Sallie was also cheering for Osinski. "Esco! You know better," she was saying, under her breath! Every time Esco bucked, Osinski stopped him. Sallie was worried that Esco wanted to harm the coach.

Under her breath, Sallie said, "Esco, if you hurt this trainer, I am going to spank you when we get to the horse trailer!" She loved Esco, but he was behaving like an out-of-control jerk, and that was a disappointment. She was impressed at how clearly Osinski remained emotionless and maintained his professional composure on the back of this fireball. Suddenly, the fight went out of Esco, and his bucking and rearing stopped. He stood motionless. Osinski tapped Esco's side with his leg, and Esco took a step forward. "Good boy!" Osinski patted him. He tapped the horse's side again, and when Esco responded, Osinski continued patting him and encouraging him. The two walked a lap around the arena, and then went into the trot, then canter. Osinski rode calmly and confidently. He had clearly gained Esco's respect.

She was impressed that Osinski rode out the fight in a dressage saddle, which, unlike a Western saddle, has no horn to hold on to. Osinski had the patience and the confidence to wait out Esco's tantrum and the skills to do so safely. She had watched the whole little show, nervous that Osinski would refuse to continue. Osinski rode Esco to where Sallie was standing. "You have a gift of an athlete here," he told her, "but he needs some work. Could you bring him down three days a week? I will ride him on two days, and you will have a lesson on your third lesson day." It was obvious that Osinski intended to school Esco in behavior, and work him to contain his energy and use it to advantage. Sallie was simply amazed that Osinski was willing to help her. And Esco knew he had found a leader in his new trainer.

By October 2008, Sallie had also continued to grow more comfortable in her career and had a good month of sales. She managed to close a few real estate transactions. Of course, the usual tag team was in play. First, Chayce, then Michael checked her work, before she would send it to her broker to get his approval. Then she would take it back to her clients, assured she was accurate in her work. But she could sense a 'cooling in the market'. The real estate market seemed to match the weather.

CHAPTER 5
HOLD YOUR MOMMA'S HAND

It was a cold to the bone, rainy, cloudy day. The horse trailer was already hooked up to the truck. Sallie asked Chayce, "Hey kiddo, why don't you come with me to my lesson?" Chayce looked left out of life a bit. His eyes lit up as he answered, "Sure mom!"
Sallie went to get Esco from his stall, while Chayce jumped in the cab of the truck, and began looking for music on the truck radio.

As she opened Esco's stall, there he stood, impatiently waiting for her. "I know Esco. Here buddy, let's get your halter on." She said. Esco as always, gently lowered his head and placed his head right in the halter. As she was fastening his halter, she could hear Chayce clearly had found his favorite song, Collide by Howdie Day, yet again. She could hear his young voice singing loudly and passionately, "I worry your face light up again. Even the best fall down sometimes. Even the wrong words seem to rhyme."

She found herself humming to the song, as she loaded Esco in the horse trailer, checking and double checking the trailer door, making certain she closed and locked it correctly. She walked up and opened the driver side of the truck, music pouring out of the cab. "Chayce! Hey! Chayce!" she spoke loudly over the radio as she turned the volume down "Hey….Aw mom! That is my favorite song." Sallie did not even acknowledge it, as she said, "Hey….I need you to come check the trailer door for me. I checked it. But I need to make sure it is locked." Check and recheck had become the routine.

This was something Chayce had become quite used to, double checking. His job was to make certain she did things correctly. He popped out of the cab, ran back to the trailer, opened the door, walked in….looked at Esco, and checked the length of his lead rope fastened to the trailer tie. He checked the half hitches in the rope, making sure Sallie did it right. He said, "Mom, you did a great job tying Esco. He's safe. The trailer door was locked and safe too. Good job!" And he slammed the trailer door closed, and latched it, and put the pin in at the top of the door.

They both hopped back in the cab of the truck. Sallie and Chayce pulled off the farm and made their way to Osinski's barn. The drive, as usual, was silent in communication between the two. Chayce turned the radio back up and found another favorite song; Bubbly by Colbie Callait. Sallie was amused hearing his young voice, "It starts in my toes. Makes me crinkle my nose. Where ever it goes. I always know. That you make me smile. Please stay for a while now, please take your time where ever you go." Though he was slightly off key, his voice had a a joyous, youthful, happy ring to it.

Hauling the horse trailer was hard on Sallie. She could drive, but it was a struggle hauling the horse trailer. Chayce's singing was actually bringing her some much needed comfort. Her peripheral vision was impaired, though she was totally unaware of it at this time. All she really knew was that, as cars passed her, it was unnerving to her that she could not see them right away. She always went the speed limit. However, cars, even in rural areas, never seem to want to be behind a horse trailer.

As she made her last turn into the driveway of Osinski's barn, her muscles would all release as if saying, "Whew we made it." She took in a deep breath and let out a large exhale. Then looked over at Chayce and said, "Thank you for coming with me." Chayce in his youthful voice, answered, "Your welcome mom. You did a great job!"

"Hey Chayce, I am going to go get Esco tacked up. She sensed the horse's moodiness and knew he would be a bit of a pill. The understanding between Esco and Sallie was unusual from the day she had met him, and his eyes had locked onto hers. He had walked up to her, with purpose and intent, chasing other, older stallions away from where she had stood at the fence, claiming her for himself. Since that day, the two were connected in some mental and spiritual way. "Why don't you sit here until I get him groomed and ready to go in the arena." Chayce, asked, "He seems fine. How do you know he he's being a pill? Are you sure you're not just afraid?" Sallie answered, "I just know."

Sallie took Esco out of the trailer and tied him to the side of it, so she could groom him and have access to the tack room in the trailer to reach for all the brushes, hoof pick, saddle, saddle pad, bridle and splint boots, the usual routine. Esco was tied to the side of the trailer; he danced and pranced. Sallie said, "That's enough Esco." And Esco decided it was more work to dance around, so he stood quiet as she picked his hooves, and then brushed his body. He stood quietly as she placed the saddle pad on his back, followed by the saddle. Last but not least, it was time for his bridle. As always, he lowered his head, picked up the bit out of her hand, and she then finished fastening up his bridle. As she led Esco, toward the indoor arena, she motioned for Chayce to follow.

All three walked into the arena.

Sallie told Chayce he could sit quietly on the mounting block during her lesson or stand by Osinski's chair. As most kids will do, he wanted to push some boundaries. With a snap of her finger and stare, she told him, "No! You stand there. No further. Or not only could you get hurt, so could I." Chayce did quietly stand and sit. Sallie began to lunge Esco, who had some energy to burn off. After a few moments, Esco became attentive taking the walk, trot, cantor cues on the lunge line. And…..Esco knew Osinski had arrived. He could hear his vehicle pull up. His ears shot forward, and he had turned his head to the door. When his eye caught sight of Osinski, he began to lick and chew. Sallie started to notice Esco could sense Osinski. And sure enough, there was a familiar, " Good afternoon!

"Hi Esco. Hello Chayce! You came with your mom. How are you?" Chayce liked Osinski, and he liked that someone noticed him. "Hi Coach! I am good. I came to support mom." Osinski smiled, "Hello Sallie, how are you?" Sallie smiled and answered, "I am well." She never really felt well. She was always in pain somewhere. Her throat would constrict, her jaw was in pain and clicked all the time, her shoulder was in chronic pain, she was exhausted all of the time in the afternoons and needed long naps, but every one kept saying she looked good and was doing well. So she figured that must be the right thing to say. "Ok", Osinski said, "Esco? Are you doing well?" As he was hooking up the ear phones he placed on her ears, connecting them to his microphone, Chayce answered for Sallie, "Esco's always good. He just chill axes and wants carrots. You know horse stuff." The comment made both Sallie and Osinski laugh.

"Ok, Sallie, let's see what you've got" Osinski said. While asking Esco to walk on a 20 meter circle around Osinski, he noticed Sallie's contact with the bit in Esco's mouth was not there. Her reins were long, slapping Esco in the face. He said, "Shorten your rein Sallie. More. You shorten your rein more. " Sallie's fingers were still so clumsy, she still couldn't grip well, but she would shorten the rein. Then Esco would nudge on the bit and the rein would rip through Sallies clumsy hands. This was a vicious cycle he noticed. She did it every lesson. Osinski used every analogy he could think of.. " Shorten the rein, feel the weight of his head in your hands"..." Use the rein as if you were shaking someone's hand.".... Sallie fumbled and fuddled with the reins. Osinski could see the effort, but she just wasn't able to make contact with the rein to the bit so Esco could feel the necessary contact.

As Chayce sat on the mounting block, Osinski quickly observed him. Then he said to Sallie, "Ok, shorten the rein...you are no longer holding a rein in each hand. You now have the hands of two little boys. One in each hand. And you will see Esco raise his head above the bit. That is him squirming, much like a little boy saying to their momma', ' but I want to go run over there so let go of my hand. I am a big boy.' But you, you keep the rein short, so the bit can have contact with his mouth, just like you would with two little boys hands, keeping a soft, gentle, yet firm grip, like you're asking Esco to just hold your hand. And Esco is pulling on you, but you just say 'No running out in traffic today Esco, you just hold my hand '. Esco did squirm, he did pull on the bit, he did want to run....he also wanted to stop.

In this very moment....Sallie remembered her oldest son Rian and she, holding hands, running down the ocean beach, both laughing and jumping waves and telling him, "Don't let go! You must hold my hand". Suddenly, Esco stopped and decided he did not need to trot any longer. And, he was rather insistent about it; he just refused to move forward. Osinski, said, "And you get him forward! He does not get to just quit. You use that whip, along with two quick kicks with your legs, tap him and tell him," Come on! Get up here!" As Esco did pick up the trot, Sallie did let go of the reins. They were quite long. Osinski said, "And gently, quietly shorten your rein, and you feel Esco's mouth just like you felt the hand of a little boy." Suddenly, another vision came to her. Sallie remembered the time she drove to school with a little boy who, once they got out of the car, laid flat on the ground like dead weight refusing to go to kindergarten. And she remembered actually having to drag him into the school, as she could not pick him up and carry him; he was as stiff as a board and impossible to carry, and she was demanding," Don't you DARE make me let go of you, or you will smack your head on the this sidewalk! You ARE going to school today Mr.!" That was her youngest son Chayce. For the first time in 9 months, she finally remembered Rian and Chayce were her sons. It was an ah-ha moment. It was the very first time she fully remembered both of her sons for who they were.

She vividly remembered her sons when they were younger, and her role as their mother. "Momma, is Michael a bad guy or a good guy", a five year old Chayce asked. Before Sallie could answer, her 11 year old son Rian hollered to Chayce, "Chayce don't be stupid. Of course Michael is a great guy. Chayce yelled out, "Momma! Rian called me stupid!" "Rian, don't call your brother stupid." Rian looked at Chayce and said, "I won't call you stupid again. But I am moms' favorite." "Chayce immediately screamed, "MOM!!!!! I knew Rian was your favorite!" The fight was on, Chayce slapped at Sallie's leg. Rian shoved Chayce to the ground yelling, "Chayce! Don't hit mom! Not ever!" Chayce swinging his little fists at Rian, who was several years older and a foot taller, yelled, "She's not your mom, she's my mom!" "BOYS!" Sallie yelled sternly, "ENOUGH!", as she grabbed each ones hand and marched them right to the couch, "Now then, you two sit here in time out. Look at me. Both of you. Do I have your attention? You will sit here and hold hands! Do you hear me?" Both Rian and Chayce answered in a muttered tone, "Yes". Chayce asked, " But momma? Why do we have to hold hands. I hate Rian." Sallie snapped, "Because you two are brothers. And you are BOTH my sons. BOTH of you are my favorite. And I love BOTH of you. When you fight and argue with each other, it takes a piece of my heart away, because I love you BOTH. You will sit here, hold hands and think until you can find one nice thing to say about each other. You can give me your answer when I come back in here. And! if either of you break hands….you're both going on restriction." Chayce, immediately calculating if the risk would be worth it, asked, "Restriction from what?" Sallie stomped her foot, "Chayce! Enough! Quiet. Not one more word!" Later she returned to the living and asked them, "Alright you two tell me one good thing you each love about the other." Chayce answered, "I love Rian because he is my big brother." Sallie smiled at Chayce, "Good job." She looked at Rian, who, six years older than Chayce, struggled to answer, "I like that Chayce is good at cleaning fish." Sallie giggled. " Ok. Good job Rian. You two are free. No more fighting! You're brothers! You will be friends! " Both boys giggled and answered, "Thanks for freeing us mom!"

As she collected the reins slightly in her hands, she and Esco continued to move around the arena. It was a good vivid memory of both her sons. She found peace in knowing that she now fully remembered the two of them in great detail. And she remembered striving to always be a good parent. Osinski finally directed Sallie to stop, and talked to Sallie about the lesson and the one to come. They were done for the day. "Alright, Esco, let's get you loaded in the trailer." she said, as she was opening the trailer door. Esco jumped right in the trailer, proud and happy of his work under saddle. "Ok Chayce, lets go home!'

Chayce and Sallie, for the first time, in nine months, actually had an in depth conversation on the ride home after this lesson. They discussed specific things they had done years before. And, as his mother, Sallie, elated, could answer his questions. "Was I a good baby?" and many other questions he had. It was also the day......he burst through the door with great pride and yelled out, "Dad! Moms back! Mom is back! Esco and Osinski, they gave me mom back!"

As 2008 was ending, driving to lessons was becoming more of challenge, not less! Most of the time, Sallie would drive to the barn feeling anxious. She didn't want to be late, but also, she didn't know if her eyesight was good enough for driving. There were many things causing her to feel unsure. She still didn't know, then, that she was experiencing light sensitivity or the effects of blind spots in her vision. Cars would pass her, and that was terrifying! She still didn't realize that she had diminished peripheral vision, either, so a car's sudden appearance in her field of vision would continue to startle her. When she drove she would see everything, trees, cars, telephone poles, lanes and lines, four ways stops, coming at her all at the same time. The was no space between her and the stimuli coming at her. Everything seemed to come at her large and in her face. She was also very concerned about hurting people in a driving accident. She was driving a big truck and huge horse trailer among the much smaller cars on the highway, and increasingly, careless drivers would pull out in front of her causing her to slam on her brakes and Esco to slide forward in the trailer. Sallie could feel poor Esco bumping into the trailer wall. She became highly vigilant about her own driving and watchful toward other drivers, but she continued the drive to the barn for her lessons under tremendous pressure.

After her lessons, Sallie would be exhausted but would feel empowered. The energy made the drive home much easier than the drive to the barn. It was clear to her that the lessons were working. At the same time, lessons, driving, gas at an all-time high, doctors' appointments, horse feed, mortgage payments, and Sallie's diminishing income were all taking a huge toll on the family. It didn't help that the economy everywhere had taken a huge hit. Real estate sales were hit especially hard at this time, which of course, was Sallie's economic contribution. Dark clouds were filling Sallie's horizon.

By December 2008, Sallie and Michael had run out of money. She took a last lesson with Osinski, and at the end of it told him she could no longer afford to continue.

"I have to close a deal or sell something," she said. "When I get more money, I will e-mail you." Osinski was very kind about it. As Sallie was walking Esco out of the arena, feeling very empty, but talked to herself, saying, "It will be okay. We'll get through this." Osinski came after her. "Hey—do you work every day?" "No, winter time is really slow in real estate." "How about you tack and groom for me, and I will train you and Esco in exchange?" Sallie was surprised and elated; suddenly it was going to be okay! "Really? That would be amazing!"

The arrangement was just what Esco and Sallie both needed. Osinski would put three rides a week on Esco and give Sallie one lesson a week in exchange for her grooming and tacking Osinski's horses. So that is what they did. Sallie would make the drive with Esco four days a week, beating the odds with white knuckles, praying to get there safely. She would get Osinski's horses out, groom them, tack them up and hand them off to him. He would hand off the horse he had just finished, and she would take the horses back, clean them, groom them and put them away. Being around Osinski's horses was healing for Sallie. She had fully remembered her sons and who she fully was. But she still struggled remembering why she married her husband Michael, and it was taking a toll on her.

One thing Sallie had become aware of was sure to cause issues, so Sallie had to mention it to Osinski. She had become aware that she would take things. She wasn't sure why, but if she had something in her hand and someone distracted her, she would just walk off with whatever she was holding. It was not only annoying, but embarrassing! She didn't mean to do it! So she stopped Osinski for a moment to tell him. "Osinski, I need to tell you. I don't know why, but I take things. I'll be holding something somewhere, and the next thing I know it's in the truck. He laughed and said, "Okay. Thank you for letting me know." Sallie didn't think he believed it. But soon it would become apparent. The next day Sallie walked into the locker room. Osinski popped in the door and began to open his lockers, saying, as he always did, "Good morning Sallie!" "Say, I've just gone through my lockers, and I can't find George's splint boot. Do you know what we did with it the other day?" Sallie's eyes opened wide, and she exclaimed, "Oh! It's in the back seat of my truck. I'll go get it." When she returned she asked, "Remember yesterday I was holding them in my hand when you were reminding me what time to show up today? Then you left." He just looked at Sallie. Then she said, "I just followed you out and then got in my truck rather than put them away, Sallie quipped. "I don't know why I do that." Osinski just looked and her again, then chuckled and said, "Okay. Let's go get the horses and get them lined up." Sallie continued to have these misadventures, but this just seemed to stop about a month later.

The horses at Osinski's barn were quiet and well mannered. The work was physical, which somehow quieted her mind. The endless questions racing through her brain, what really happened; why did Esco fall, why could she not remember, why had she married Michael, why could she remember a career before her sons., was she going crazy, did some undiagnosed mental illness show up, plagued her constantly. Her coordination was improving, the memories continued to become more clear, but driving was a constant struggle, the light sensitivity was painful and her jaw pain was getting worse and worse. But the horses, they did not seem to be bothered by her one bit.

2009

CHAPTER 6
RE- CONNECTING

In January 2009, one night after dinner, Chayce had gone to bed. Michael and Sallie were watching the T.V. She looked at Michael, trying to remember why she married him. All it seemed he had done the past year was say, "No. No you're not. Oh no you can't". In addition to the accident, of which she still had no memory, she had no perception of how injured she was either. She was sure she was not injured anymore, in spite of the vision issues, driving issues, continued and worsening jaw and other pains. She was trying to understand why she would marry someone who told her "no" all the time. There were very little conversations between her and Michael. And those that did happen all seemed to end in one answer, "No". Everyone in Sallie's life all spoke highly of Michael. "What a gift" he was to her. However, she absolutely could not remember anything that was magical or gift like quality in him. She still was unaware of any of the things Michael had done and was still doing for her. He had been silent about it for nearly a year.

On that particular evening, she sat on the couch, moving her wedding ring on her finger, staring at it. As she moved it with her fingers, she asked

"Why did I marry you?" The question did not surprise Michael, for he had anticipated that this moment would arrive at some point in time. He, sat quietly for a moment, and then turned off the TV. He paused for a few seconds, gathering his thoughts, and then answered her by saying, "You married me because I was the love of your life." Sallie, internalized those words, "Married you because, I was the love of your life." Those words did not seem to fit anywhere within her being. Looking at the wedding ring, she slipped it off her finger and held it in her hand. She asked, "Did we do anything together? Did we ever talk?" Michael answered, "We did lots. And, you did the talking." She knew there was a wedding, and she could vaguely remember marrying him. She just could not remember for what reason. And she could not remember who he was as a person. She took the ring in her hand, tossed it to Michael and said, "I want a divorce". Michael remained in his chair, quietly starring at the ring, as Sallie walked toward the door. Once again he found himself drawing on the many times he had considered this moment might come. He looked up at her and softly said, "You think you do huh?" Sallie answered back, through her tear stricken voice, "Yes, I do. I don't remember who you are, and all you do is tell me "No". Tears now streamed down her face. She found herself exhausted in thought nearly daily trying to remember the details of who people were in her life and thought this might make that struggle a bit less complicated.

Michael maintained his calm, quiet demeanor, then rose up from his chair and walked over to Sallie. He reached out to her softly, then gently took for her hand and slid the ring back on her finger. It was in a calming voice that he said, "I had suspected you did not remember me. But, I think you will in time." Sallie looked up at him with tears streaming from her eyes, and asked, "But what if I don't?" Their eyes came together in that moment as Michael drew her close to comfort her. Then he said, "I can live with that." He held her as her tears soaked his shoulder. She asked him, "Why did you marry me?" Michael took in a deep breath then released a long sigh. This time however, that sound she had found so annoying seemed to bring comfort to Sallie. He drew out the handkerchief that he always had in his pocket, and as he wiped her tears away from her cheek he answered, "I married you, because you were the most sincere, open and honest person I had ever met. Your smile, there has always been something about your smile that warmed my heart. "

Sallie looked up at Michael and said, "Well I believe it must have been a cold heart." Michael was momentarily taken aback but then chuckled as he said, "It probably was, but you melted it." It was in that moment that, for the first time in nearly a year, Sallie felt a slight sense of comfort from Michael as he continued to hold her in his warm embrace. It was the first time in nearly a year there was any kind of familiar feeling toward him. Randomly and out of nowhere she said, ' I love Esco." Once again Michael could only laugh as he replied, 'Oh I know you love Esco." A short time later Michael appeared with some picture albums that Sallie had put together herself. They were remembrances' from the first year they were married. She had no recollection of seeing the photographs before; in fact she didn't know where the albums had come from. However Michael and Sallie finished the evening at the kitchen table looking at old photographs. Some photos sparked a memory. Many others did not. But the two were becoming friends once more.

Hauling Esco to Osinski's barn four days a week was a continued challenge for Sallie. Her horse trailer was an old, steel, dark blue contraption that could hold four horses. She was grateful to have a way to get to her lessons with Esco, and she knew hauling was her way to what seemed much needed relief. She had recovered memories of hauling the horse trailer all over the States of Washington and Oregon. She truly could not understand why driving in general was so difficult for her now, much less hauling a horse trailer. She still found herself surprised by cars that seemed to appear from nowhere in the lanes next to her. It was becoming increasingly terrifying to her. But again, she enjoyed the work with Osinski once she would get to his barn. So she thought, "All I have to do is go a little further, and then there is a sense of peace." She would tell herself this mile marker after mile marker, corner after corner, as she would trundle down the highway that took her to his barn. She had had many conversations with Michael about getting a smaller trailer, but it was obvious to Michael that she was much better, and after all, she had driven that thing all over the country before.

Once she would arrive at the facility, Sallie would feel a sense of relief. She enjoyed the work with Osinski and the lesson's on Esco. Her balance and coordination were continuing to improve as each month passed. She was gaining ground on Esco through her riding, as well as gaining confidence in her personal life. She had regained a good sense of herself and who she was. With each lesson Osinski gave her on Esco, it stimulated memories of who she was in her core being. Osinski gave her home work in her riding to practice on Esco in her own arena on the days she was not at his facility. This kept her active, as it gave her goals that were attainable to achieve, as well as kept Esco working hard and in line. And the grooming kept her connected to Esco, lessons, and Osinski. Though no one realized it, the grooming was an exeptional form of occupational rehab.

February, 2009, provided new challenges for Sallie. It would become mentally harder for her to want to ride Esco, and the month also brought an increasing sense of fear. She could not understand why, but she did know, if she did not continue to ride every day, it would be much like learning to drive again. If she did not drive every day, even just to drive around the block, it was as though she had never driven before.

Michael and Chayce continued to give their full support to her. Both were home more than they had ever been before the accident. Michael was an avid outdoorsman. He had not been fishing or hunting a single time since the fall. One February day, Sallie got up, and both Michael and Chayce were scurrying about the house gathering up their heavy clothing for fishing. She started getting dressed and ready to make her way down the hill to her home arena to ride Esco. Michael stopped her at the door by saying, "Where are you going?" Sallie answered, "To go ride Esco, of course!" Michael answered, "But Chayce and I are going fishing." Sallie laughed and said, "Go fishing! " Michael found no humor in that. "We are going fishing. You need to wait to ride." Stunned, but determined Sallie responded, "Good! Go fishing! I am going riding! You can both show me your fish!" Michael and Chayce, both, were quiet in their activity as well as in demeanor. Sensing a building frustration in him, Michael asked, "Hey Chayce? The net is in the garage. Why don't you go get it and put it in the back of the truck." Chayce happily skipped out the door saying, "On it dad!". Michael understood Sallie's need to ride; he had been witness to the changes that it brought to her. However, he also knew that he had to paint a very clear picture if she were to see the risk at hand. He took a breath, and then calmly said to Sallie, "Hey, you almost died last year. Had I not been here the day Esco fell, you would have died. He almost killed you! He did everything he could not to rollover on top of you. But had I not been here to get you breathing again and call the ambulance, you would have died. Please, just please will you wait to ride, until Chayce and I return from fishing? Can you do that?" Sallie stood silent like frozen statue, with the words piercing her to the core of her soul. "You almost died. Had I not been here, you would have died." No one had said those words to her before. In that moment Michael's words painted the clearest picture of just how severe her accident had been. She looked at Michael, both stunned and bewildered as she said softly, "yes. Yes I can wait."

As Michael and Chayce finished loading up the truck with tackle boxes and fishing poles, Sallie observed the smiles on their faces, the joking and laughing both Michael and Chayce were exchanging. She waived to them, "Have a great time you two!" As Michael was backing up the truck, he said out the window, "Thank you, we won't be gone more than a few hours. You can ride at noon. We will be home by then." She still had no concept of how her accident affected the lives of those closest to her, she just didn't get it.

Sallie was left at home alone with her thoughts while Michael and Chayce went fishing. "You almost died. He almost killed you!" Those were words that had never been said to her in the last year, but as she sat on the back deck that over looked the arena, she began to recognize the seriousness her position. The sun peeked out of the clouds on occasion, and the barn stood out brown and red against the green pasture around it. The arena beckoned to her, but would remain silent. She sat on the porch deep in thought. It was as though she was caught in a web. Some things did start making sense to her as she reflected back on the last year, such as why either Michael or Chayce always insisted one or the other had to be right in the middle of the arena as she rode. She had not really been aware before, but she suddenly realized, clearly, that neither of her guards was ever more than 20 feet away while she was riding. And as she looked around the farm in that moment, she was grateful she was still alive. She thought about both her sons. She was grateful to still be here to watch her youngest son still grow up. She laughed to herself with a mother's joy as she thought about his smile, his jokes and his singing. She was also grateful not to just remember him, but to get to really know him as a person.

She sat there, lightly rubbing the back of her neck, stiff and still burning with pain.. She was aware that her shoulder, she was constantly shrugging it in small circles, always felt hot and tingly and was always so stiff. She touched her jaw, persistent with a sharp burning pain. She sat still, processing that she almost died the year before; the burn down the spine from the base of her neck came and went. It lit up again as she rubbed the front of her neck, trying to rub it away. She lived in tremendous physical pain daily. She had brought it up in her doctors appointments, medications were often discussed. But Sallie had many allergies to different pain medications. One thing was clear. She had noticed every time after she rode Esco, the physical pain seemed to be less, significantly less.

Suddenly, Esco nickered to her as he could see her sitting up on the deck, "I know Esco," she answered. Esco stood still, staring at her. He quietly nickered to her again. "Soon Esco, we will ride soon!". Esco stood quietly to her response, standing in the sun with his brilliant copper coat catching the sun. As promised, Michael and Chayce returned right at noon. The fresh water trout were laid in the sink, and Michael followed Sallie to the barn so she could ride Esco. As Sallie rode, Chayce remained in the house to clean the fish he and his dad had caught.

It was April 2009, about fourteen months after the event, spring was in the air and Esco could smell it. Everything was green and fresh from the rains. Flowers were beginning to bud and bloom in the Northwest, turning the landscape brilliant in many colors. Spring to stallions means one thing and one thing only, breeding season. Sallie and Michael started their day in the arena. As Sallie walked up the mounting block to mount Esco, she knew this ride was not going to be pleasant. He was full of energy, puffing and prancing, antsy by any standard. She sat in the saddle. Esco immediately puffed up, blowing and snorting as she rode him. She could feel the power of 1200 pounds of muscle. His coat glowed with a deep iridescent, reddish- copper sheen and the definition of his massive neck was beautiful. She could not feel his feet touch the ground for the 20 minutes she rode. She gently asked Esco to give him the left side of his jaw and then the right. She was riding a keg of dynamite, and she knew it. But by the grace of God, he settled down and there was no explosive reaction from Esco.

Sallie's experience and intuition told her that Esco's actions were not a once-in-a-blue-moon occurrence. She had seen this before. Perhaps there was a bit of uncertainty in her own confidence to control Esco, but she now believed that the stallions growing strength and maturity, his need to dominate, had to be corrected immediately. She looked at Michael and said, "I need to geld him." The statement came as a complete surprise to Michael. He looked at her while saying, "No, he has not done a single thing wrong. You can't geld him. You had a plan. We made a business decision when we bought him. Do you remember?! You're not gelding him". She dismounted Esco, tossed the reins at Michael and with a great intensity said, "You have him fall on you, and then you ride him! ." She left Esco with Michael in the arena and stormed up the hill to the house. This would be a new tension between Michael and Sallie.

As spring 2009 went on, Esco was behaving more and more like what he was, a young stallion wanting to establish himself. With each ride, there was more and more "puffing" up, like the proud soul that he was. The proud, vibrant stallion behavior made it increasingly harder for Sallie to want to ride. In the back of her mind, since Michael had told her, was the nagging specter that she had almost died. The trips to Osinski's barn were becoming more and more intense. Esco would be pounding around in the horse trailer. The force of his movement would shove Sallies' truck toward the oncoming traffic. She would be exhausted just from the forty minute haul to get to Osinski. At that point, Esco would often be a handful for her to tack up, as he wouldn't relax, and the hormones racing through him made him unpredictable.

Following one such trip to her lesson, Sallie found herself at the mounting block, preparing to get on Esco. She looked at Osinski and said, " I just don't know. I just don't know anymore." She took a deep breath and mounted Esco, and Esco vibrantly and proudly pranced, puffed up in full stallion fashion. Osinski went right into coaching mode, "Sallie, take a feel of his mouth. Tactfully, take up rein that's right…a little left, and little more right. Just gently massage his mouth, flex him to the inside of the ring….good and to the outside…..good. Sallie I do understand. It is hard to ride him when he is like this. I don't particularly like it either."   Esco was somewhere in between wanting to behave and wanting to breed during the ride. Sallie still was not able to feel his feet touch the ground,   because he was so full of testosterone and barely in control. She just could not take it. It did not just make her fearful; she seemed to completely shut down. She could not hear, she could not see. She would return to that place she was immediately after the accident ,'trapped somewhere between space and time', unaware of her surroundings, unaware of what she was doing. This would last several minutes. And then, she would return back into the world of awareness. She could sense Esco was in a place mentally where she knew she could at least stop him safely and dismount. And that is exactly what she did. She looked at Osinski with pleading in her eye.   She shook in her core, her stomach turned and churned. Osinski walked up to her, taking the reins to Esco.   "Alright Mr. Esco, come on."   As she watched, Osinski mounted Esco from the mounting block. He made it all look so easy, so controlled. As Osinski rode Esco on a 20 meter circle around her, he asked, "You doing ok, Sallie?" A few moments of pause went by before Sallie responded, "Some days, I just feel so small, so pathetic." Osinski looked right at her as he rode Esco and said, "You don't even know all the power you have. You have no idea do you?"

It was in that moment that Sallie started to realize that she had no clue. She felt unsure how to move forward. And she knew she was losing ground with Esco. She said, "I ....I want to geld him. I need to geld him. Had he never fallen, ok, I could ride this out. But......Osinski he fell. How can I ride him when I cannot even feel his feet touch the ground?" Osinski finished the ride on Esco before he responded. "Sallie, I have seen many stallions in my career. Esco is a good boy. But he has testosterone overload. He's not dangerous yet. But it is coming. It's all in there. I agree with you. Geld him. Sallie responded, "I wish I could." Osinski said, "Why can't you? He's your horse. Sallie answered, "My husband Michael does not agree. I wanted to geld Esco before the accident. He was a handful, though he did really calm down. It's also written in Escogido's purchase and sale agreement that I will not geld him." Osinski compassionately listened and professionally said, "I understand. But Sallie, he's fallen on you. And you got real lucky. Why risk it?" Sallie said, "I made a promise. I promised I would never geld him. I bought with the understanding his breeding would help cover expenses. I promised Michael." Once again, Osinski compassionately and professionally responded, " We all think that with Stallions. I can ride him Sallie, and I can take him out and show him for you your first year. We can see how he does. I am willing to help you. You talk it over with Michael and keep me posted."

The rides at home on Esco were becoming increasingly difficult on Sallie as well. Even with Michael in the middle of the arena, Esco would become irritated and upset during the rides, and Sallie would question her ability. During one particular ride on Esco, Sallie told Michael, " If you like me at all, please stand on the outside of the arena." Esco used his front leg to strike out at Michael as he walked by, to which Michael said, "Esco you're an ass." As Sallie put Esco back to work, Michael could see Esco's feet were over 3 feet off the ground. It was spectacular to watch. To ride it however, was an entirely different picture. It took all Sallie had, mentally, emotionally and physically, as she gently asked Esco for left side and right side. Again she could not feel his feet on the ground. It sent a chill up her spine. For over 20 minutes, she kept Esco going. And she finally could not ride any longer. She knew she was about to go to the land of "trapped in space and time", that place where she went when she just mentally checked out. She asked Esco to stop, and prayed that he did so with no explosion. She dismounted, and this time she said to Michael, "I am gelding him this week." Michael answered back, "He's fine. He looked great. He was just fine. What is wrong with you?"

"What is wrong with me? You have this fucker fall on you, and then I want you to get your ass back up on him and ride! " Sallie spoke in a quiet but deadly tone, and then she caught herself in disbelief. She ripped off her helmet, threw it at Michael, who ducked. She had thrown it with such force, it split when it hit the rail beyond him. Michael picked up her helmet, which had cracked with the force against the fence. Sallie went and put Esco in his stall. As she untacked Esco, she grew more frustrated with Michael. She finished and turned Esco out in his paddock. Finally, she marched up to Michael with tears streaming down her face and she said, "What's wrong with me? You said I almost died. Last year! After asking you for almost a year what happened, you refused to talk about it. And I am riding a horse that almost killed me. I am grateful to still be alive, to still be here at all. To see both my kids grow another year. This horse is becoming dangerous as a stallion. It's only my life up there. I am not riding him to die! I ride him to get better! Why I even have to beg to geld him in beyond me. Divorce me if you have to. I am gelding him this week!"

Michael sat quietly on a rail at the arena as Sallie walked back up the hill to their home. He stayed there for quite some time pondering all that she had said. While their family's financial situation was still perilous at best, Michael realized that jeopardizing Sallie's safety in hopes of recouping some of the investment they had made for the stallion was untenable. He returned to the house, whereupon it was agreed that Esco would be gelded that week.

Esco was gelded, and while her riding lessons were progressing nicely, the family's financial matters continued on a downward spiral. Sallie had been unable to close a real estate deal in months. The cost of gasoline for her truck had become outrageous, eclipsing five dollars a gallon and still climbing. Feed and hay costs had also sky rocketed and many in her community were feeling the pinch. However, to those around Sallie, it appeared that she was now completely functional in life. Her enthusiasm for real estate was strong and the confidence in her skills was intact. Even Sallie's brain was telling her that she was completely functional, but her body told her another story. She could walk and talk, but was still experiencing tremendous anxiety when driving and had a great deal of constant, nagging physical pain. Because of these challenges it had become apparent to the couple that they could not sustain their current course. Michael told Sallie that, while their finances were very tight, change was possible if Sallie would consider changing jobs. The real estate market had completely crashed and like many real estate brokers, she had no clients and no prospects. She now understood that she needed to find a different job; and Michael's support left Sallie feeling much more confident in life.

CHAPTER 7
FATHER'S DAY

Father's day was approaching and Michael gave the instruction; no gifts that cost money. He reminded Sallie, "Finances were tight." though it wasn't until later that she would learn that a mountain of debt was accruing interest at unsustainable rates that would destroy the family's finances.

Sallie went down to her barn to ride Esco. Esco was on the pushy side with her that day. He was irritable; he was not respecting her space. However, he was not the defensive stallion he had become before he was gelded. He grumbled to her as he nickered. As she held Esco at the mounting block, she caught a glimpse of Chayce coming down the hill from the house, "Mom, dad said I need to be down here while you're riding." Sallie paused and yelled to Chayce, "That's fine. Don't run down the hill please; I am getting on." Chayce made it in a brisk walk to the bottom of the hill, before Sallie put her foot in the stirrup and got on a willful stubborn Esco. The second she sat on Esco's back, he was tossing his head as if saying, "Come on! What are you going to do about it?" Sallie, sat up tall, doing her best to stay right in the middle of Esco's back. Esco again, tossed his head up high as if saying, "You have no idea what I am capable of." For the first time, Sallie used her dressage whip. She tapped him firmly on his on his shoulder, simultaneously kicking his sides with her legs, giving Esco the reprimand and cue to walk on. Esco, refused to walk forward. He just stood stubborn as could be. Sallie again cued him with her legs, and Esco reared. Sallie had no choice, but to reprimand him again, this time with a little more intensity. Esco licked and chewed, and as she gave her cues with her legs again asking him to walk on, he calmly and obediently did so like a gentleman. Once he was warmed up in the walk, she asked him with her leg cues to pick up the trot. Esco again protested. It was clear this was a pattern for this ride. Again, Sallie had to reinforce that she did mean business.

After a few sneezes from Esco, and a lick and chew, he followed her cues and picked up the trot. Sallie worked Esco in the trot for only a few minutes. When he stopped and reared again, she really got after him saying, "Escogido! You are going to find out exactly what I am capable of. Gets your ass moving!" After that discussion, the ride went quite well, Esco behaving and following her cues. As the ride finished, Chayce, who watched the ride said, "Mom, you sounded like you were talking to dad" as he laughed. Michael, laughed with Chayce while saying, "I know Esco. I have learned not to give her too much hell. She always wins." And Sallie felt proud of herself that she had ridden it out.

She was used to hearing things like this the last few months or so, but had no idea what it meant. Always wins what? She asked herself silently, as she cooled Esco out in a walk in the arena. She caught a glance of Michael's face and his genuine smile. In that very moment, she finally remembered something familiar about Michael. It was an old argument with him! He had come home, and was still in uniform, while Sallie was making dinner. He did the usual, came in the kitchen gave her a hug and kiss. She said, "Hi babe, the garbage is full. Can you take it out so I can finish making dinner?" Michael answered, "You take it out." She firmly said, "Michael! Take the damn garbage out! I am making dinner." Michael stood there, in shock and let out a Freudian slip, "You just really have no idea all that I am capable of do you?" Sallie rolled her eyes and answered back, "You might arrest bad guys on the street, however in THIS house there are no bad guys. And, YOU are going to find out exactly what I am capable of if YOU don't take the garbage out! I am making dinner!" Michael stared at her, and like a little kid, lifted the filled garbage bag out of the garbage bin, walked it out the door, and put it in the dumpster. The image and the conversation were another one of those moments that just seemed to come out of nowhere as her mind worked to repair itself and she worked to reconstruct her life.

Sallie dismounted Esco and walked him back to the barn to untack him. While taking Esco's saddle off, she vividly remembered meeting Michael and all their phone conversations. As she brushed Esco, she recalled all the fishing trips, motorcycle rides, the marriage proposal, the wedding, the roles they both played in their marriage together.   Deep in thought, while she put Esco's saddle and bridle away, she suddenly felt a real sense of who Michael was. "Ready to go up to the house?" she asked Michael and Chayce. Both Michael and Chayce laughed, "We are ready...are you finally ready?" She smiled, reaching out her hand to Michael, "Yes, I am ready, let's go." The three of them, Michael, Sallie and Chayce all held hands while walking up to the house for dinner.

After dinner, Chayce and Michael cleaned the kitchen and the two were watching TV. Sallie asked Michael, "Where are all the photo albums?" Michael said he would bring them in from the garage. He brought in three large boxes of photos. Sallie spent the entire evening until early morning looking at photos by herself. Each one, she now recognized. Every single photo with Michael in it, she fully remembered being there. Many photos were of hunting or fishing trips. She stumbled across a photo and recognized that was the day Michael proposed to her. She was sitting in a fishing boat, wearing her engagement ring. She came across another photo of Michael in his S.W.A.T. uniform. The photo reminded her of a night a few months after they were married. Michael had been called out for a SWAT Call. As he was getting dressed in the middle of the night, Sallie got up with him and made coffee. She watched him as he had made several trips to his patrol car taking all his SWAT gear. His last trip out was with his rifle over his shoulder. He gave her a quick kiss while grabbing his coffee. As he was heading out the door, she said "I love you. Have a good night." Michael had a serious look on his face as he answered, "Love you too." Then she quickly asked, "What is a good night for you?" Michael, impressed she took the time to ask, answered, "Not getting dead and coming home to you." He flashed his brilliant full smile that he rarely did for anyone, and quickly went through the door, loaded his rifle in his patrol car and drove out of the driveway.

Sallie remembered! It was in that very moment her eye's had been reopened to the dangers of Michaels career in Law Enforcement. As she stood there, watching the patrol car leave, she made a promise to herself. She would never be angry every over any reason with Michael. She would also keep her words sweet, in the event something ever did happened. She remembered she had never wanted to regret saying words in anger that she could never take back.

As she looked at more photographs, the details of her marriage became very clear. Michael was a strong willed personality, but loving and kind, a stable person and deeply loyal spouse. He was not home often, due to his career. On his days off, he often went hunting or fishing depending on what season it was, to decompress from the dregs of society he often encountered and the tension of the conflicts he would encounter on the job.

As Sallie continued going through all the photos reminiscing, she realized what a gift Michael really had been to her life., helping raise two sons that were not his own blood, but who he did not treat any differently than if he had sons of his own, attending numerous football games, baseball games, taking them on adventures of motorcycle riding, hunting and fishing trips. She felt a deep love and appreciation for Michael and his devotion to her sons. As Father's Day was approaching, Sallie put together a small video of she and Michael's life together. It was her way of showing him she really full remembered who he was. Michael was moved by the video and felt a sense of relief things would eventually be back to normal.

CHAPTER 8
HURDLES AND INTERRUPTIONS

Michael Kowalski and Mike Osinski had one thing in common, Sallie had noticed. Neither one had to raise his voice to command respect. Osinski let Esco know his misbehavior was unacceptable and began to show the horse what his job was. It was several months into 2009, and it appeared to everyone Sallie had regained full, functional control of her life. Even to Sallie, she felt fully functional. The riding was good. Osinski was a perfect trainer, though she was still having tremendous anxiety when driving, and she was still in a lot of physical pain. But she could walk and talk. She was confident again with the real estate career. It appeared her skills were back intact. The real estate market had completely crashed however. Like many real estate brokers she had no clients and no prospects. She understood she needed to get a job; Michael made it clear to her things were very tight financially, but would be just fine if she worked. And Sallie felt much more confident in life. She had been riding with Osinski, Esco was doing great under his instruction, and so was she. Everyone was oblivious to the setbacks to come.

Sallie again had to deliver the news to Osinski that she had to stop her riding lessons. She had begun seriously job searching, but things had changed since 2004, the last time she had had to change careers. Instead of looking at job listings in the newspaper, she found she had to go "online". "Go to WorkSource," her friends said, or "Look on Monster." Sallie did her best, but going online to find a job was baffling to her.

Luckily, an insurance company that Sallie had interviewed with prior to her accident was still interested in hiring her. Sallie went through the interview process again, and this time she completed it. She was hired. She would have to go through testing to earn her insurance license, but she had recently succeeded in completing her real estate clock hours, so she didn't expect any problems. It took her three tries to pass the test. "What is wrong with me?" Sallie would ask herself. "I finished the entire real estate course and passed the exam in three days in 2004. How can I possibly be this stupid?" She had immersed herself in studying. She was still sleeping a lot, but after every nap, she'd return to the course materials. How could she not pass the test when she was studying so hard? Finally, after three attempts, she passed one section of the course but had still not passed the second section. Sallie decided to ask for advice from the man who had hired her. The company had switched managers, and the one she spoke with wasn't the one she was originally going to work with. She hoped the new manager could help her.

"I'm really struggling with this," she told him. "Do you have some tips for me? I don't understand why I'm struggling so much. "Her supervisor looked at her. "Tell me someone you admire. "Sallie didn't have to think about her answer. "My grandfather." She perked up. The manager must want her to emulate her grandfather's success. However, that wasn't what he had in mind. The manager raised his arms and rested his head in his hands. "Your grandfather?" he asked with a hint of sarcasm. "What did your good ol' granddaddy ever do?" Sallie was taken aback. She had worked hard and asked for help, and now this supervisor was belittling her admiration for someone she loved and looked up to before he bothered to listen to "Why" this man was such an icon for her. She knew then there was no way she would work for him. She didn't need to raise her voice. "My grandfather did more than you'll ever achieve in your lifetime," she said. She got up and walked out the door. Soon after, she sent a letter of resignation.

A few days later, Sallie visited her friend John and prior employer at his new job. As with many in the industry, John had closed his own company when the market fell out and taken a job as a loan officer at a bank. He gave her a big hug when he saw her. John had always known her to be aggressive and a work horse. In fact, she was his only loan officer to do as much in volume in sales as he did on several occasions. She looked sharp and gorgeous as she always had. After she left John's company to move into real estate, she had called him numerous times to discuss prospects and check his perceptions. John had been a long standing mentor to Sallie. When she had called him to check out the job market, he had told her, "come on down!" The bank he worked for was looking for someone with all her talents, and he knew she would be perfect in the position available.

"How are you doing? Where have you been? Pamela and I miss you." He hadn't heard from her for quite some time. John looked over at the bank branch manager he worked with and called out to her, "Sallie would have no problems going into businesses and talking about our bank services." He knew nothing about her accident or the problems she had had trying to regain a foothold in her life. You look great! How have you been doing? How are the horses?" John had given her a big hug and chatted about home, horses and how tough the housing market was. Horses had given them one more thing in common and created a lifelong bond. To John, they were just picking up where they had left off, and he looked forward to working with her again.

The bank had been looking for someone to fulfill the role of Relationship Manager. John made introductions. Sallie spoke with the bank manager and found she really liked her. By the end of the conversation, the manager had asked for Sallie's resume. The bank's hiring process would take a couple of weeks, she was told, but she had the job.

It was a relief, in July 2009, to be formally offered the job at the bank. After Sallie had met the manager and interviewed, the job and the manager had seemed to be a perfect fit. Though Sallie was still fatigued and sleeping through much of the day, she and Michael thought it was because she had not had scheduled work days and a work week, that she was just unused to the change in routine. She thought she was just suffering from having been lazy for so long. She didn't put together that each Osinski lesson was followed by complete exhaustion and afternoon naps. She didn't seem to understand that driving, alone, was an exhausting enterprise that had been plaguing her since her accident in 2008.

The bank manager was lovely, and she assured Sallie that all she had to do was get through some training modules, all done online. Surely this seemed it would be a "walk in the park. But again, Sallie struggled. The training modules were tiny, yet Sallie could not retain the information. She tried to concentrate by sitting in the back room of the different bank branches she visited as she introduced herself, going over and over the training modules, but learning the material was taking too long in Sallie's estimation. At the home bank, Sallie's manager wasn't helping. She and

Sallie had a great relationship. She was fun and easy going, but she would pop up over the wall of Sallie's cubicle to chat, and it interrupted Sallie's concentration. Sallie would struggle after each interruption to refocus. She couldn't understand why she couldn't refocus. She had always found it easy to multi-task before. This time, Michael was noticing her exhaustion. Sallie would come home from work at 6 pm, walk in the door, collapse on the couch, and sleep until six the next morning. Even with this much sleep, he could physically see her fatigue. He knew this was dangerous and was growing concerned. She had come so far, personally and in her physical recovery, and it seemed that this fatigue would derail her progress if not corrected immediately.

Finally, Sallie had to acknowledge that she simply couldn't do it. Something was not working with in her brain. She couldn't even articulate why she couldn't get through the training modules. Her coworkers were friendly and enjoyed having Sallie on the team. In fact, one of her jobs was to help motivate the morning staff. She could talk about creating personal relationships, how to treat customers, and how to increase sales and productivity, but she couldn't learn the details of the products the bank offered. She knew she wasn't meeting her responsibilities, which wasn't acceptable to her ,and she refused to blame anyone else for her failure to learn the material. Within eight weeks after starting at the bank, Sallie quietly resigned. Something was wrong, and she didn't know what it was.

While Michael and Chayce could see her struggle, her co-workers couldn't. They called her to say they'd miss her. The president who handled the retail side of the bank's business phoned her as well, to let her know she would be missed. Sallie was moved by the phone calls of appreciation, though privately in her mind, she knew she had failed. She could not read and remember the bank's products well enough to be of service to new clients.

In her mind Sallie considered herself a failure, and none of it made sense. She had always been quick to learn anything having to do with Finance and Banking products within the industry. Before her real estate career in 2004, she was a commercial and residential lender for over 15 yrs. It was a market she knew very well. In fact, she read and memorized all information in her real estate course in 3 days in 2004 and passed her real estate state exam on the first try. For heaven sake, working with the lending industry, she had memorized the 200 lenders her broker was approved with and could immediately respond to a question about any of the products offered by each. She was perplexed with herself and deeply frustrated as to why simple training modules with the new bank's products and services where this difficult.

She went to the only place that gave her comfort and perspective it seemed, and that was to Escogido. As she was tacking him up, Michael said to her, "It seems like all you want to do is ride Esco. Sallie we need you to work." Sallie remained silent. She took Esco to the mounting block, and got on him. The ride was a hard ride. She felt an overwhelming sense of fear. Esco also sensed her fear, which caused him to be hyper vigilant. He started looking for things from which to protect her. A leaf, was now cause for him to be on high alert to protect her. After all, Sallie was terrified. The leaf must be a predator, as he struck the ground fiercely with his front leg. Esco was unique. He was an Andalusian, known for their loyalty to their owner. Horses, no matter the breed, are fight or flight creatures. Most flee at perceived danger. Esco fought it. He never ran from anything. He was a loyal soul and fiercely protective. That was just enough for Sallie to decide to end the ride. She quickly jumped off Esco's back. As she held the reins in her hands, they were shaking. She led Esco across the arena to take him to the barn and untack him. Michael asked, "What's wrong? Why did you jump off him so fast?" Sallie felt like life was closing in on her. "I don't know why Michael." she said nearly lost. She quickly untacked Esco, gave him a quick brush down and turned him out in his paddock as she always did.

As she passed Michael to make her way up the hill that led back to their home, Michael asked again, " Is there something wrong?" though he already knew the answer. Once again he had seen her downward spiral coming and was searching for a way to engage her to learn more of what she was experiencing. Sallie shouted, "I don't know WHAT's wrong with me." Michael tried to reach for her to hug her. She flung his arm off her. "Something, there is something wrong with me. I don't know what it is." As they continued to walk toward the house, Michael was deep in thought, considering all he was seeing and hearing from the woman he loved. It was difficult to watch her suffer through the anxiety that clearly gripped her life. After all, he was a fixer. It's what he had done and done well throughout his career. Yet now, he had no answers, no direction to help steer Sallie away from the challenges that were overtaking her once more. During the ride he just saw, Esco was not behaving badly. Though he struck the ground with his front leg, Michael had watched Sallie ride through much worse than that over the years he was married to her.

As Michael entered the house, he saw Sallie in the kitchen getting a glass of water. Michael said, "We gelded him months ago. He seems to be in a better place. So what did he do today that was so bad? " Sallie stood in the kitchen drinking her water, silently looking out the window. She turned and faced Michael, "There is something, I don't know what it is. Something is wrong with me." Michael asked, "Think you should go back to the Dr.?" Sallie stood thinking about all the times she had been to the Dr. the past year. She looked at Michael, "I've been to the Dr. All I hear is how wonderful I look, and how great I am doing." Silent tears fell down her cheeks; Michael took out his handkerchief and began gently wiping them away. "I need a lesson." she told him. Michael's heart grew heavy. He would gladly give her the world if it was within his grasp, but lessons cost money and that was something they no longer had. He looked at her saying, "A lesson? You just quit your job." Sallie stared out side again looking over the farm, and quietly said, "It just looks like I am riding a horse. But, something...there is something that happens when I ride in a lesson vs. when I don't ride in one. I don't know what it is. But it makes me better. I can think better!" "Something......there is something wrong with my thinking now. I don't know what it is exactly. But that coach, he sees it. I struggle! I struggle just to ride. Just to drive to the lessons make me feel like I am losing my mind! And lessons are a thing I love, so it's not avoidance behavior. There is something wrong. That coach has seen it, though. He sees it! Esco sees it; he senses it or something. The Dr. says I look great and am doing well. But something is SO wrong. I don't know what it is. If it's one thing or 20 things. I don't know! When have I ever not worked? Answer that Michael? When have I ever just decided to NOT work! Something is wrong!" she shouted. The tears burst from Sallie's eyes once more, "Perhaps I have some mental illness now. They said it was just a concussion. I have had a concussion before! You know that. It was nothing like this. Who the fuck forgets their kids! What mother forgets her kids! What wife forgets their husband and best friend! Who does that?" She screamed.

Michael stood in front of Sallie, softly embracing her in an effort to calm her down. His mind drifted back in time, remembering she did have a concussion right before they were married. He had taken Sallie and the kids to Beverly Sand Dunes. It was March 17th, 2001. He remembered her sitting on the back of the motorcycle trailer. She had just taken off all her riding gear when a man lost control of his dirt bike and drove frantically through their campsite, flipped his bike over the motorcycle trailer that Sallie was sitting on. As the rider cartwheeled over her, the foot peg of the motorcycle as well as the steel toe clip to his boot caught, her in the back of the head. It was a bad accident for sure, Michael thought, but she had not forgotten who he was, nor her kids. He remembered her body was heavily bruised. Her petite frame looked like she had been beaten. She had large bruises up and down her legs, neck and arms. In fact, one leg was bruised so badly, it was a few weeks before she could put her full weight on it to walk normally. But she had not let such serious injuries slow her down. She was back to work, kids, school, and horses in a short time.. He also remembered the doctor saying that the blow to her head had concussed her pituitary gland so hard, she had acquired something called Addison's Disease. And with that recollection, a new perspective of the scope of Sallie's injuries was gained by Michael. Even if he couldn't see the injury, he now realized that, whatever it was that was causing the mayhem in their lives, it was as great as any injury they had known. It was with a new sense of compassion that, Michael walked over to Sallie, who was now staring out the window again. He wrapped his arms around her waist and kissed her head. "Go ahead and make an appointment for a lesson."

So at the end of September 2009, Sallie called Osinski, and on October 1, she put Esco into the horse trailer and headed to the facility. As Sallie drove, an image suddenly flashed through her mind. She saw her trailer smashing into the back of her truck and decapitating her. It was not only a vision, but something she could feel. Something in her neck since the accident made her jaw burn sharply, agonizingly, and it seemed as though she could feel something cutting through her neck. Anytime Esco moved in the trailer, the trailer would move against the hitch on the back of the truck.

The nudging, bumping motion would bring on a fresh horror— flashes of the trailer slamming into her. Sallie could feel the bones around her eye socket move with each nudge on the trailer into the hitch, moving the truck. Within a few more miles, Esco would slam in the trailer, and the trailer would slam on the hitch, which was slamming the truck. She could feel her neck; it seemed to crack and pop with the motion of the truck, sort of bobbing loosely on her neck. And as she would try to loosen her shoulders, the muscles in her jaw would tighten causing a loud "pop" in her jaw. Little did she know, the combination of it all was creating the perfect storm. Not only was her body feeling terror now, the sound of that jaw popping in her head was so loud, with each and every push from the trailer to the truck, she started seeing flashes of being shot in the head. She would try to relax her jaw by slowly opening it. The "Pop" from her jaw joint would coincide with the flashes of being shot in the head. If she would try to lift her shoulders, her neck would pop so loud, along with her jaw popping again, more flashes of being shot in the head would build with intensity.

After forty unnerving and exhausting minutes on the road, Sallie arrived at the training barn shaking and drenched in sweat. Somehow she managed to hold herself together, tack up Esco, and get ready to ride. "Trying to shake it all off, she muttered to herself, "It's just some bizarre avoidance behavior or something you're doing to yourself".

Over the next couple of weeks, the day terrors intensified. Suddenly, every time she drove, the fear of being shot in the head stayed with her, no matter where she went.

Her neck and jaw pain became increasingly intense, and her jaw would make a popping sound. That "pop" sound in her head transformed into a bullet entering her skull. She was shot … and dead. Pop… shot…dead. Pop… shot…dead. Over and over, her mind repeated the scene. The pain was tremendous, a burn shooting through the side of her face.

Sallie and Michael lived next to Fort Lewis, a military base, which added to Sallie's overwhelming fear. They could hear the volleys of heavy munitions, loud booms in the distance, from soldiers practicing their skills. She began sleeping on the floor in case a bullet might come flying into the house. She was afraid to drive anywhere near Fort Lewis, much of the lands surrounding Sallie and Michaels farm,, and that made getting to her lessons an intimidating challenge.

Sallie didn't tell Osinski or anyone, about these new fears. She thought she must be insane. She knew the scenes flashing through her mind weren't normal, that people don't usually see such images. She relayed these incidents to Michael, not Chayce, but Michael didn't respond. Being a pragmatic man, he knew the chances of Sallie's nightmare coming to fruition were near impossible. Then, too, he considered that by engaging those fears it might lend more credence to her internal torment. He said nothing and just took it all in. She finally told him she was thinking about going to see a psychiatrist and he agreed that might be the right thing to do.

The fears and scenes continued to intensify, so persistent that Sallie signed on to the Internet to check for a shrink. She had serious concerns that she was mentally ill. She found Psychologists and came across the name, Doctor David Monson, PHD. His list of specialties included Anxiety, Depression and Trauma .

Clearly this psychologist was qualified and capable of giving Sallie the mental illness diagnosis that she was sure she had. So she picked up the phone and called him, "This is Doctor Monson", he answered. Sallie in a professional voice said, "Hi Doctor Monson. My name is Sallie Stewart, and

I am fucked up. I need an appointment." There was a pause on the phone. "Well honesty and candor don't appear to be an issue for you. I have a full calendar right now. Why don't you tell me a little about what is going on." Dr Monson answered. "I, I had this accident. My horse fell on me. Now something is wrong with me. I think it gave me a mental illness. They say it was a concussion… but I think I have gone insane. " Sallie answered. Again, there was a pause. "What are your symptoms? Meaning what are you experiencing?" Dr Monson asked. Sallie gathered her thoughts for a few seconds, "I have this tremendous fear now, especially when I drive. It's horrific. I shake. I physically shake when I drive now. It was one of the reasons I just quit my job. My husband is upset about it, my son is frustrated…" The doctor interrupted her sentence by saying, "You know you're in luck. I just had a cancellation. Can you come in this week?" Relieved, Sallie agreed to the appointment.

On October 15, 2009, Sallie met Dr. Monson, her new psychologist. He first asked her what concerned her the most. Sallie didn't have to think about it. She blurted, "Fear! The fear when I drive or haul the horse trailer." He laughed and looked at her, "Horse trailer?" She filled him in about her mounting fears: of driving, and her increasing fear of riding her Esco, as well as her increasing fear of being shot in the head. After listening to Sallie's account of her accident and the months that followed, Dr. Monson asked her if she dreamed at night. She replied, "No". He then explained her symptoms matched the criteria for post-traumatic stress disorder. He claimed that because Sallie didn't dream at night to work through her issues, she experienced day terrors instead of nightmares. And because she had no memory of the accident or the six weeks following it, her brain was manufacturing the fearsome scenes. The good news according to Dr. Monson, was that aside from her PTSD, Sallie was mentally healthy. Sallie didn't believe the doctor that she was sane, but he assured her that she had no mental illness. He told her that she had PTSD, which was a condition due to a traumatic event and that it was very treatable. He encouraged her, telling her that she should continue facing the activities that created the flashes. He told her that for each one she faced and pushed through, they would decrease in frequency and intensity. He asked her if the flashes ever showed up on the horse. Sallie told him she never had a flash on the horses back. But she did feel more anxious before riding. She asked him how to get through the fear. He replied "when fear shows up say, "Hi, fear. Thank you for showing up. Sit right here. I will let you know when I need you!" He continued saying fear was a good thing to have, but that she must learn to control it. He said that fear was what protected people in back in cave man days. People felt fear and ran from danger. She just needed to learn how to control it.

Dr. Monson recommended that she continue to ride Esco, as riding Esco, was desensitizing her. It was a clear connection for the Dr., an impartial person on the outside listening to her. It was clear in his view that riding Esco, the horse who had fallen on her, was an incredible way for her to desensitize herself and handle stress. He explained to her that PTSD, was something that, if faced would get better. Each flash episode she experienced would get better, if she did not give in to the episodes by stopping what she was doing. Since they were happening so much while driving, he suggested she not back down. He told her, "Stay your course. Don't stop, don't have someone come get you, don't quit driving. Push through it. You can pull over, but don't abort the trip" She suffered, still, from the over stimulation of everything zooming at her. She couldn't yet go into Costco, or stores for the same reason. And it seemed to be worse.

Learning to desensitize herself and handle stress helped Sallie calm down a bit while driving. She was still unsettled by her fears, and her family life still seemed out of her control, but at least now she understood why the flashes were persisting. And she could talk through it, and the fear did substantially decrease. Then, just as Sallie was beginning to conquer her fears, something happened that made them all too real for her.

Two weeks after Sallie first met Dr. Monson, October 31st, 2009, her world was turned upside-down by a premeditated act of horrific violence. Seattle police officers, Timothy Brenton and Britt Sweeney were sitting in their patrol car at a quiet Seattle intersection. It was Halloween night, normally a time when Police Officers focus their attention on watching out for and interacting with little ghosts and goblins searching out sweet treats. For most officers, these few hours after sunset are a pleasant distraction from their normal duties. But on this evening everything went terribly, tragically wrong. A car slowly pulled alongside the parked patrol car. Without warning, the occupant of the moving car raised a gun from inside his car's window and opened fire. Neither officer had any warning before several high caliber projectiles burst into their vehicle. One round ripped into Officer Brenton, fatally wounding the officer instantly. Officer Sweeney was grazed by another passing round as she rolled away from the incoming fire. And with that, the car drove away into the darkness of Halloween night. Neither Michael nor Sallie knew either of the officers attacked. However, there's a bond that connects all law enforcement officer and their families, and in that moment, all of Sallies silent fears emerged from deep in her brain. Brenton was 39 years old and married with two young children. He had spent nine years with the Seattle Police Department, and his father and uncle were retired police officers. The similarities between Officer Brenton's family and her own were undeniable. The incident hit hard for both Sallie and Michael. For Michael, it was a stark reminder of the dangers police officers face, and the impact they have on those that surround each officer. Making this even harder to comprehend was that

Officer Brenton had been assassinated. He was targeted for wearing a uniform while sitting in a police car. The attack could have happened to any one of them. That same fact did not escape Sallie, but as scary as the incident was, Michael was in Detectives at the time and not working the streets, and that provided some small sense of relief to Sallie.

What also helped bring comfort to Sallie were Osinski's riding lessons. The family finances were crumbling, but Sallie still had Michael's commitment to the lessons and that gave her something to look forward to. From Dr. Monson, she was learning that what had happened to her—having Esco fall on her—was not a normal experience. The doctor encouraged her not to fight her fear, but rather master it. To continue to ride Esco and face him is what would help her PTSD more than anything. Officer Brenton's murder remained prominent in the media and in her thoughts. However as sad as it was, it had no immediate impact on her psychology. It was, however, a wakeup call for Michael. Michael was a detective and did not work the streets consistently, but the event set off some alarm bells and served as a preview of a new challenge to come for Sallie.

It was Sunday, November 29, a typically cold, wet and gray Puget Sound morning. It was mid-morning when Michael's cell phone rang before going to voice mail. Then his work cellphone started ringing repeatedly. Michael was not working that day and was outside doing farm chores. Sallie was in the house when the calls shifted to her own phone. In a short time, Sallie found herself taking call after call from people, coworkers asking, "Is Michael there? Please have him call." Sallie instinctively knew something was wrong and ran outside to look for him. When she finally found Michael, she told him all of their phones had been ringing off the hook. The house was literally echoing with rings from all the phones. Michael immediately recognized the urgency of the moment and ran back to the house. One of the calls came from a retired Police captain who had worked with Michael. He had terrible news; four police officers had just been shot and killed in Lakewood, Washington, a city close to his own jurisdiction.. Recognizing the enormity of the situation, Michael assembled his gear and readied himself for duty. However, as the day progressed, it became clear that the investigative resources of Michael's agency would not be dispatched to the scene. None the less, Michael and Sallie spent a very long and unsettling day in front of their TV watching the news.

Once more, the details were shocking. The four police officers; Sgt. Mark Renninger and Officers Tina Griswold, Gregory Richards and Ronald Owens were at a local coffee shop completing reports on their laptop computers when a man, not known to any of them, entered the store, then walked up on them from behind. Without so much as a word, he opened fire on them. Three of the officers were shot dead immediately. The fourth officer engaged their shooter in a physical struggle before succumbing to a gunshot himself. And just like the events in Seattle one month earlier, the gunman turned and walked out of the coffee shop without comment.

The Lakewood Four, as these officers would come to be known, died just miles where Michael worked. The two police agencies often worked together, and there were many friendships, both professional and personal, between their staffs. While the killing of Officer Brenton had been shocking enough, this act of incredible brutality was as severe a blow to the entire region as any experienced. Once again, the killer was someone who's hatred of law enforcement officers led him to assassinate these people without reason or warning.

The impact on Michael and Sallie's life was immense. The phone calls made by co-workers, friends, and family to the family's home didn't stop for weeks. People were beside themselves, horrified, outraged, and heartbroken, and so were Michael and Sallie. The reality of the danger that Michael's profession presented was crashing down on the couple in a manner they had never experienced nor anticipated. The murders prompted a great deal of soul searching for both, as they tried to understand the random nature of the attack. All of these officers had families, three of them had small children, and those parallels were not lost on either Michael or Sallie.

While upset by the seemingly unending chain of events, Michael found some solace in the confidence he'd developed through training he had received over the years. He had undergone what he referred to as "old school" training, with officer safety and situational awareness deeply ingrained in him. If he had to focus on writing reports, he would pick a strategic location where no one could come up behind him. The tragedies had their effect on him and would change him forever. The possibility of being targeted became an ever present consideration in his mind, and Michael would spend a lot of time checking his rear and side view mirrors and watching the people near him.

At home, the family didn't talk about the killings. While public outpouring of support was constantly on display by the media for weeks, both Michael and Sallie were trying to silently move through the events. What they felt most of all was tremendous compassion for the surviving spouses and children. Sallie had seen Michael and other law enforcement officers deal with loss before; violence was a part of their landscape. They would process their grief and move on out of necessity. But this was different. The enormity and brutality of these murders was something no one had ever experienced. Sallie made herself available if Michael needed anything, but what seemed most healing for him was to go hunting and fishing more often. Sallie knew he needed to get out in nature and decompress.

The one who demonstrated the greatest reaction to the traumatic events was Chayce. Because so many officers had been shot and killed, Chayce no longer wanted to go places with Michael or be seen in public with him. Since Sallie's accident, Chayce's relationship with his mom had changed. He had grown closer to his dad in the early days of Sallie's recovery, and now he was afraid he was going to lose his dad. He also had some fear he would become a target too. As parents, Michael and Sallie frequently reassured him that it was ok to be seen in public with his dad. Chayce would counter by saying, "I don't want to go to dinner with you and dad" or "someone might recognize him. He's a target now it feels like."

With so much happening around them, Michael and Sallie didn't really have time to "feel", or process their own feelings, as a couple. Grief and anger were palpable throughout the community, and the killings seemed to be the only topic of conversation where ever they went. The weeks following this tragedy saw a succession of tributes, fund raisers, public and private events and remembrances, culminating in a public Law Enforcement Memorial Service that required use of the Tacoma Dome to accommodate all the mourners. It was on December 9th when the community gathered together to honor the Lakewood Four in a public memorial service. Michael and Sallie got up before dawn on a freezing morning and climbed into Michael's patrol car. Despite the fact that the car's heater didn't work, the two endured twenty degree temperatures as they drove in a several mile long procession with surviving family members, other law enforcement personnel and community members to Tacoma Dome. Huge ladder trucks from the fire department lined the route, American flags had been suspended between their ladders.

In spite of the sadness borne from this event, both Michael and Sallie found consolation in the supportive messages displayed from the thousands of people lining the streets: "Thank you for your service." "We love you. Gone but Not Forgotten." Michael and Sallie could feel their grief transformed into love and concern for the fallen police officers and their families. It was a powerful experience for them both.. At one point, all the police cars stopped. On each side of the procession stood rows of people, watching the long line of police cars pass by, and crying. Sallie waved at the spectators, and they waved back "Wave to them," she told Michael. He sighed, for he was used to negative reactions from the public. "Michael. All these people are here for you. Wave your hand at them!" He did, and the crowd burst into cheers, waving and clapping their hands. Michael could feel their compassion and appreciated it.

Once the procession arrived at the Tacoma Dome, the couple walked into the arena, joining police officers from all around the nation as well as Royal Canadian Mounted Police. There were more than 20,000 people in attendance inside the building, and despite the frigid weather, thousands more stood outside. The floor and upper levels of the arena were ringed with television cameras and crews, prepared to broadcast the service live to the Pacific Northwest region. The Tacoma Dome is a huge place, but it suddenly felt very small to Sallie. She and Michael walked by the four coffins, each one draped with an American flag and accompanied by a photo of the fallen officer.

The service was a sad, but fitting tribute to the four officers. Dignitaries addressed each as a hero, with Washington Governor Christine Gregoire noting "We will remember them today, we will remember them always". Sallie was able to hold herself together until the three children of Officer Greg Richards provided a beautiful tribute to their dad. Later that evening, Sallie entered a comment on her Facebook page. "Grief brings us gifts. Those are the love and compassion to those who grieve." In conversation with others, Sallie would remember thinking, "what a legacy Greg Richards has left behind with his amazing children". The entire crowd, some twenty thousand people, could not contain their emotion for there was not a dry eye inside the auditorium.

Watching the family, Sallie felt she could relate to them. Standing next to her was Michael in his Class-A uniform. The two of them drew comfort from each other and the thousands of other law officers that surrounded them. In front of them were the four, flag draped coffins, where Sergeant Renninger, and Officers Richards, Griswold and Owens rested for the tribute. Sallie and Michael really had no thoughts until the children spoke. They were simply numbed by it all. Sallie found the memorial service beautiful, powerful, and gut wrenching all at the same time. It was different for Michael, serving as a reminder that no one is invincible. When it was done, it was late into the night and both were spent. Sallie, who still needed a lot of sleep, was exhausted. Once inside the car, her patience for Michael's courtesy, letting every one of the thousands of cars exit the Tacoma Dome's parking lot before he would move, quickly disappeared. Fatigue and the cold were getting to her. "We have absolutely no heat," she hinted, thinking it might prompt him to start moving. "That's a fact, the heater in this fine department car does not work," he replied. Shivering, Sallie drove her point home by saying: "Michael, is this going to be the headline tomorrow? 'Puyallup police officer and wife found with frozen snot sickles stuck to their face, frozen to death in car'?" Michael laughed. "God, I hope not!" "Come on, mister!" Through chattering teeth, Sallie commanded "EVOC", a reference to his pursuit driving instruction. "Get us the hell out of here!" Michael revved up the engine and started their drive away, their laughter at her demand and use of police jargon helping to ease the tension as they drove home. They passed by many memorials and candlelight vigils taking place throughout the area. The mourning would be a long process for the officers and their communities.

Chayce had stayed home from the service because he was sick, and Sallie and Michael found him sleeping on the couch with the television on when they returned home. Sallie, still wearing her heavy coat, went into the kitchen for a glass of water, and Michael went into the living room and sat in his chair. Not quite awake, Chayce struggled off the couch and staggered sleepily to sit with Michael. The boy reached up with his hand and turned Michael's face to him. "Dad, are you going to die?" Recognizing the concern and sincerity of his son's question, Michael drew his face close to Chayce's, placing his nose against his son's. "No," he said. "I'm too mean to die". That seemed to comfort Chayce, and he and Michael held on to each other. Over his head, Michael and Sallie locked eyes. While the public service signaled a transition in the mourning process for the public, the impact of this tragedy on Michael was unchanged. He became more focused on the tactics he used in his job, honing a strong sense of situational awareness. He also began working with Sallie on defensive tactics and maneuvers, quieting his own concerns about her safety. As a defensive tactic instructor at the police department for 10 years, he knew what to teach Sallie, so she could compensate for her still weaker left side.

Tragedy was not ready to leave the Puget Sound Law Enforcement community. On December 21st, two more Pierce County law enforcement officers were shot. However this time the circumstances were different. Sgt. Nick Hauser and Deputy Kent Mundell had responded to a home in a rural area of the county, when they were shot trying to remove an unwanted guest at the request of the homeowner. The house was located near the small town of Eatonville, only 17 miles from Michael and Sallie's home. The gunman initially agreed to leave the home with the officers but produced a gun and fired on them as they were leaving the residence. Both officers were struck, but Deputy Mundell was able to return fire, killing the gunman. Mundell was critically injured in the exchange. With no regard for her own protection, the gunman's 15-year-old daughter helped to drag the wounded officer into the protection of an adjoining bedroom before running to a neighbor's house to call for help. Sergeant Hausner was treated for his gunshot wounds and released on Christmas Eve. Sadly, Deputy Mundell succumbed to his injuries when he was released from life support on Dec. 28.

It was like déjà vu. Only two weeks earlier, Michael and Sallie had walked out of Tacoma Dome, exhausted and but glad they had been part of the largest law enforcement memorial ever assembled in the Pacific Northwest. Knowing that the brutality of a law enforcement murder was a rare event, the couple thought they would never have to attend another funeral like that for the rest of Michael's career. They were wrong. The grieving cycle would start again and the events of those two months in 2009 would stay with Sallie for a long time. Along with celebrating the holidays, she and Michael would remember the fallen officers. Sallie came to believe that these events were not something to "just get over," but that they became a part of her, and she would learn to carry on. It was part of the inner strength, which was good to know as things were about to get personally worse.

CHAPTER 9
DISCOVERY

Sallie continued to meet with Dr Monson PHD, and he continued to encourage her to ride Esco. This was a welcome attitude, as other people in Sallie's life were not in favor of her riding. "Are you considering taking the continued risk of riding?" family members would ask. And her doctors were telling her she could never get hit in the head again—not ever. And not just in riding. But never hit her head again. Not falling down the stairs, and not in a motor vehicle accident. Doctors were very insistent that another blow to her head of any kind could kill her after the hit she had sustained. The news was not helping her PTSD by any measure. "Try living in a world where you cannot sustain an accident, ever." she would often think to herself, as she was driving. And it seemed just as she had that thought, some irate driver would cut her off in traffic, nearly causing an accident.

Sallie had a much-anticipated lesson with Osinski shortly after Sergeant Hausner and Deputy Mundell were shot. She and Esco had been improving steadily under his guidance. That day, though, Sallie was frozen at the mounting block. The day terrors were no longer limited to driving, but seemed to have moved to Esco's back. She would have horrific flashes of Esco falling on her while riding him. In her mind, the imagined accidents were torturing her. She couldn't move. In the speakers in her ears, Sallie heard the kind but firm words of Osinski: "Get on. Get on, Sallie. Get on!" Sallie stood motionless as fear was winning, and she was losing. Osinski approached her, took the reins from her hand, gently released her fingers from Esco's mane, and got on the horse himself.

As Osinski rode Esco, he spoke compassionately to Sallie. "What's going on Sallie?" Osinski asked. She stood in the middle of the arena as he rode Esco around her. She answered, "I, I, I...I am afraid." As he continued to ride around her, Osinski said, "I know you are. Fear, Sallie is a part of life. We all have fear. All of us, as people, myself included, all experience fear. Some of us are afraid of success, some are afraid of failure. Fear is a part of life. But we overcome it. We work through it."

Sallie watched him ride a few laps on Esco before she said, "But, I am so tired of it owning my life." His kindness and calm manner was exactly what Sallie needed, and she wondered how he did it. She mused over this in another lesson. She had been able to get on Esco, and she was trotting Esco in 20 meter circles around Osinski. She hadn't yet cantered Esco for more than a few strides since the accident. It had taken a long time for Sallie to have enough balance. Her left leg still had neuropathy; her left hand still was not coordinated. She was very unsure if she could even ride a canter. Physically she had gained much more strength the past year, but how does one know what they can do until they do it? "Good in the forward trot," he said. "When you're ready, slide your outside leg back—and canter." Sallie continued trotting Esco in a circle. One lap, two laps ... six laps. "That is a lovely trot, Sallie, now canter ... canter ... Canter!" Sallie could feel her skin go pale white. She tried to move her leg, but it stubbornly stayed where it was, and tears filled her eyes. She felt so frustrated, so full of self-doubt. ' Can I even steer in the canter?' she thought to herself. She lifted her hand to her eye to wipe away a tear, not wanting Osinski to see. "Sallie." Osinski's voice was soft and compassionate in her headset. "I know—I know, Sallie, you're afraid. But you have determination, I have seen it. "His voice, still kind, grew in intensity. "Grab that determination in the pit of your gut, and ride with that determination!"

The minute she heard those words, slowly her outside leg began to move back, and Esco popped up in the canter for the very first time. "Good for you Sallie" Osinski said. "Good for you!". Sallie could only keep Esco in the canter for half of a 20meter circle. But she did it! It was a great sense of accomplishment for her. "Now, your homework is to work on cantering Esco. With your determination, I want to see you canter a full 20 meter circle Sallie." Sallie smiled as Osinski, "Well now that I know I can for sure ride it, I will! I will practice! Thank you Osinski." Sallie said with a smile.

The memorial service for the Lakewood Four had brought out the best in people, but it also brought some negative comments on social media. Sallie saw messages complaining that people in all kinds of careers risk their lives, but public response is indifferent if one of them dies. She was concerned about the anger she saw, and didn't want another police officer shot because some angered, outraged person thought they had been slighted or disregarded.

CHAPTER 10
GRIEF DOES BRING US GIFTS

As the wife of a police officer, Sallie knew firsthand how a career in law enforcement affected one's family life. She had learned in her marriage to Michael that the wife of a police officer must be strong, positive, supportive, and able to bear the weight of the world on her shoulders. The wife of a police officer keeps her words sweet and kind, mindful that the minute her husband leaves the house, he might enter a life-threatening situation. The wife of a cop gets used to hearing "I'm going to be late" and "Just go ahead without me." She forever excuses his absence from family events, never divulging details or confidential information, always just answering, "He's working" when asked "Where's Michael?" by family members. She learns to laugh at the comments made—"We never see your husband. Are you still married?" and regretfully tells her children, "Daddy wishes he could be here, but he is chasing bad guys today." The wife of a police officer learns to take much in stride and be tough as nails, flexible as gum. She learns early to be a good, strong leader. And she absolutely cherishes the times when she does see her husband. When the sixth officer within three months was killed, Sallie's heart went out to spouses, children and family members of each officer. What she understood as a possibility for her every time Michael went to work, the possibility that he might not come home, had become a reality for the family of Pierce County Deputy Kent Mundell.

When Sallie had remembered who Michael was on Father's Day, just a few months prior, she in essence got her husband back. By December 28, the wife of Kent Mundell lost her husband forever. In fact, six families had lost husbands, fathers, a mother, son or daughter. As Sallie mingled with her social media friends and family, she could see a lot of messages from people wanting to do something for the families of these officers. Many were asking her how they could help. In her life, Sallie had experienced grief that took her breath away and caused so many tears that eventually there were no more tears to cry. But she had also experienced the gifts that grief brings: love and compassion for those who currently grieve. It was the power of her friends on social media and her own grief that drove her to plan a fundraiser.

Not only did she support Mundells' family, she also remembered Bryona Crable, the teenage daughter of the shooter. According to the news, on the night of the shooting, Bryona fought with her dad to prevent him from continuing to shoot at Mundell and Sergeant Nick Hauser. Sallie believed that Bryona's actions had saved Hausner's life. She wanted to send the message that when someone does the right thing, the community will rally for that person as well as for law enforcement. And she didn't want anyone to forget that Bryona also lost her dad that night.

Recognizing Bryona's courage, Mundells' family gave their blessing to include her as a beneficiary of the fundraiser, which Sallie called "Heroes for Heroes." In less than three weeks, Sallie used her energy to start a nonprofit organization and gathered a group of amazing volunteers. She became obsessed with planning the fundraiser. She asked an attorney to set up the nonprofit. She put out a call for donations on social media. The very first people to donate items were horse people—who did not even live in the state of Washington. Within a week, auction items started coming in, one by one, from all over the United States. A high school friend of Sallie's called to let her know, he just saw the request for auction items. However, he was in South Korea and would be calling her with his list as soon as his plane landed in Hawaii. The gestures of generosity and kindness moved her. Her faith in people's good nature was being restored.

Michael accompanied Sallie to Emerald Downs, a racetrack in Auburn, Washington. After sharing her plans for a fundraiser, the managers and owner agreed to host it at the local landmark. Sallie believed it was because of their talk with Michael. Sallie slept a lot to manage her continuing exhaustion, but when she awoke at night, she'd continue organizing and sorting through the copious piles of paperwork required for the nonprofit. Just as she had struggled with the training modules at the bank, Sallie found it hard to tackle the paperwork. The attorney had done the best he could do to try to break up the information for her, but she spent hours trying to make sense of it. Michael came downstairs at three o'clock one morning to see Sallie busy with the papers and her computer. "Why are you doing all this?" he asked. Sallie gave him a challenging look. "What do you mean, why am I doing all of this, Michael?"

He paused, and recognizing the fight in her voice, chose not to answer. Sallie continued. "She lost her husband. The fact that you and I can even sit here and have this conversation… is why I'm doing this, because she can't have this conversation with her husband. She lost her husband, Michael. Her husband is dead. I found mine, but she lost hers. Now either hand me those papers and help me … or just leave." Michael did not respond, but instead, gave her a concerned look. He could see that she was not well, looking very thin and immensely tired. "Are you going to be OK?" he repeated. "I'm going to be fine if you'll just get out of here."

Detective Ed Troyer from the Pierce County Sheriff's Department served as the emcee for the Heroes for Heroes fundraiser on February 13, 2010, at Emerald Downs. The dinner and auction attracted more than a hundred people, who contributed nearly fifteen thousand dollars. A reporter from KING 5 News was on hand to cover the event, where dozens of donated items were auctioned off.

Federal Way Police Lieutenant Cary Murphy contributed a special triple-digit Seattle Mariners team jersey printed with the name "Mundell" and "423," his badge number. Chayce, who attended the fundraiser, pointed it out to Sallie. "Mommy, that jersey would be so cool. And it has the officer's badge on it. I would love to have that," he said quietly. Knowing how much Chayce had been through, Sallie couldn't say no. She bid on it and bought it for her son. Chayce later donated the jersey to the Pierce County sheriffs, who displayed it on a wall in their offices.

The money raised during "Heroes for Heroes" was divided among Mundell's children, Austin and Kirsten, and Crable's daughter, Bryona. Sallie was delighted with the event and happy with the news coverage, which she felt depicted law enforcement as a compassionate family. Planning the fundraiser had been emotionally healing for her, a way to show that she would never forget the fallen officers—those targeted because of the uniforms they wore—and their families. The previous year had been a traumatic one in their community.

2010

CHAPTER 11
TWO STEPS FORWARD, THREE STEPS BACK

During the three weeks Sallie spent planning the fundraiser, she had taken only the third week off from riding Esco. With the event behind her, she felt elated but also exhausted, mentally and physically. It had been 24 months since the accident, and she believed she had made tremendous progress—she could take care of herself and be a parent to Chayce and a wife to Michael. She could ride Esco. That is to say, she could walk Esco, and trot Esco, but not canter or work lateral movement. But her self-satisfaction wasn't to last.

Imperceptibly at first, her progress had begun slipping away. Sallie's speech was slurring more. She felt out of sorts, but she and Michael chalked that up to stress. By March, her physical symptoms were getting progressively worse. There were large blind spots in her vision. She could get confused easily, and her short-term memory had deteriorated. Her left hand didn't work well, and she couldn't read more than just a few words at a time. A single sentence was too much.

In addition, something continued to be wrong with Sallie's jaw. She found she couldn't swallow, and as a consequence, the weight was just dropping off. She still had not had a brain scan to see the extent of damage that had been done. No doctor had ordered further testing, so she was still shooting in the dark as she struggled to get better. She thought she was all healed up, but physically as well as cognitively, she was struggling more. She still had incredible jaw pain, but at this point, she had also begun limping and her balance had just disappeared. Her speech was changing, and she slurred so much people would ask her if she had been drinking. And when the exhaustion set in, which was all the time, all of these symptoms would magnify. She was unable to go in to stores because the universe would seem to come at her all at once, and the sensory stimulation would take its toll. The friends who knew Sallie before her accident were shocked began to say things like, "Sallie, My God, you are so thin, you are ungodly thin," and they would whisper in her ear, "What is wrong with you?" Sallie kept saying, "It's stress."

She remembered people who had had panic attacks. They would say things like, "I feel like I can't breathe." Sallie had never heard them say they felt like they couldn't swallow, but she thought this must be her own reaction to anxiety, like a lump in the throat. Though after the fundraiser was over, it was not that Sallie had a lump in her throat, she simply could not swallow. Food was something she would choke on. Water, became a struggle to swallow. She was very much losing in life. "Who in their right mind cannot swallow" she would think with each and every choke.

One of her friends, Chris, who had known Sallie since childhood, called to tell Sallie she had done a great job on the fundraiser. And Sallie thanked Chris as well. Her friend had offered her home as a drop-off site for all the donations that came in for the auction. Chris said, "What are you up to? What are doing?" Sallie said, "I don't know… This horse… I had this accident." "Yeah, you mentioned that." "Something's wrong and I don't know what it is," Sallie said. "What happened?" "I don't know what happened. The doctor said I had a concussion with bleeds, but I don't know. Something is wrong, though." "Well, what's wrong?" Chris asked quietly. "I don't know. Things are wrong." Sallie couldn't tell her or describe it. All she could say was that she didn't know.

"Have you been to the doctor?"

"Many time's." she replied.

"Well, what do they say?" Sallie could hear the quiet concern in Chris's voice.

"That I had a concussion with bleeds. In all my follow ups, any concern I bring up the doctor just says I must have really rang my bell." Chris was silent for a moment. Then she asked, "What further testing have they done with you? Sallie thought for a moment. "None. The doctor says I am doing great, though." "You mean they have done no follow-up tests? None at all? After two years?" "No. No tests. The doctor says I look great and I am doing good." "Well," Chris said. "You need to go back into that doctor. You need to have another discussion with him. And Sallie—you look right in his eyes this time with this discussion. You were a stallion owner. You talk to him as if he were your horse. ""OK."

On the day of her appointment in late March, Sallie she walked through the family doctors office like a powerhouse.. This time when the doctor came into the room, she greeted him like a stallion owner. She got straight to the point. "You keep telling me I had this concussion with bleeds." "Yes, that's right, Sallie," he said with a smile. One thing Sallie liked about her doctor was his cheerfulness. "Don't you think that merits a follow-up MRI?" Still smiling, the doctor looked in Sallie's chart. The smile left his face as he focused intently on the medical report. He looked up at Sallie. "Oh, I'm sorry," he said. "Yes. You were supposed to have had a follow-up MRI in April of 2008. Yes."

Within a week, Sallie was given an MRI. Her doctor called her back to his office, and this time there was no happy smile. "Have a seat. I need to send you to a neurologist," he said. "OK." "I don't know how to read this MRI. You don't have a brain tumor, and I don't think you're still bleeding in the brain." But he said nothing further about her MRI

"OK."

He said he would find a neurologist close to her home. He also ordered a Neuro-psych evaluation to determine if there were parts of her brain creating behavioral or cognitive issues due to the neurological damage. Unfortunately, the neurologist was booked out eight weeks. In the months leading up to her neurology appointment, Sallie's PTSD symptoms reemerged. When she found herself in a stressful situation or around people who were worried, Sallie became anxious. Before, she had been able to keep her cool, even if others didn't. This was different. She was beginning to truly understand she was not the same person she was before her accident.

One of the hardest situations was facing others' expectations that she could perform the same way she did before the accident. It seemed to them that she had completely recovered. Organizing the fundraiser appeared to prove that, and those around her thought it was time to pick herself up and move on. Her limitations were invisible to most, and some family members and friends didn't understand that it took her much longer to do the things she used to do, and that doing them required much more effort. These misunderstandings created conflict and stress for Sallie.

In the months leading up to her neurology appointment, Sallie's anxiety was out of control. She felt lost. New symptoms continued to emerge. She was beginning to understand she did not handle stress nearly as well as she had. Finally, her appointment with the neurologist arrived. She met an older, very dry, very curt man. He hardly introduced himself. "Come in, have a seat," he said.

"Sallie, I have read the CT scans and MRI, and I've read the hospital reports and your doctor's referral" Sallie cut him off. "What hospital records? And why?" He gave her a surprised look, which was replaced by an expression of compassion. "The date of this report looks like the date your horse fell on you, two years ago February 17, 2008" he said. "What is your understanding of that injury?" Sallie couldn't believe he was asking her this. Most people were telling her to stop talking about the accident. She was used to hearing "Get over it. You just had a concussion with a couple of bleeds. You need to move on." "I did not have an injury," she told the neurologist. "They said I had a concussion. What I can't figure out is why..." It was his turn to interrupt. "And when was it you felt part of the human race again?" Sallie was astonished. She wondered if this guy was psychic.

"Easter" she said. "It was Easter 2008, I knew."

"And when was it you knew your children?"

Sallie's jaw dropped. "Nine months..."

"And your husband?" he asked.

"15 months."

"And you, Sallie, when did you remember you?"

Tears slid down Sallie's face. "About a year."

"Well, I'm not surprised." He sat quietly, and Sallie watched him. It appeared he was mulling something over. He seemed to be grappling with some decision and trying to compose himself.

After a moment he spoke to her. "You did not have a concussion. You had a very significant injury—a traumatic brain injury. The only thing missing from your injury was a permanent coma and death." After the Dr gave her a thorough physical examination and went over her neuropsychological test results. He was impressed with just how well she was doing. He asked her, "The fact that you could physically walk in here in impressive. How did you recover?"

Sallie sat in silence, "My husband and son, got me walking and talking again. " The Dr seemed impressed with the family unit relationship. "When did you go back to work? Your records say you work. " he asked. Sallie nodded as she said, "About 7 months after the accident. It was real tough." The Dr smiled kindly and asked, "What is it you do for work?" Sallie answered slowly, "Real Estate." The Dr smiled and asked, "what did you do before real estate?" Sallie answered as she tried to clear her throat, "Lending. I was a commercial and residential lender for about 15 years". You appear to be physically fit. Do you work out?" Sallie quietly and slowly responded, "I ride." The doctor asked, "Ride? Ride what?" Sallie answered, "I ride my horse." The doctor shocked, and not happy, said, "Oh of course you do. And next you are going to tell me it is the same horse that did this to you?" Sallie, becoming used to everyone questioning her answered, "Yes. Yes I ride on Esco, the same horse."

The doctor stared at her with intensity as he said, "When was it you started to ride again?" Sallie answered, "Six Months after. I was cleared to get on. My primary care physician did clear me. He said I must ride with a helmet. My husband said I can never ride alone in the arena again." The doctor did not seem pleased, but also seemed curious at the same time as he asked, "And how often do you ride?" Sallie answered "Six…Six days a week. I have home work to practice from my coach. So I ride six days a week."

"Coach?" the doctor asked. "And what discipline of riding do you ride?" Sallie answered, "Dressage, though I'm not there yet. I'm just walking and trotting right now."

The doctor smiled a compassionate smile as he said, "I am familiar with Dressage. Sallie, I want to make it clear to you. Head trauma is serious. You had what looks like a good concussion March 17th 2001, and then, with this TBI, February 17th, 2008. Sallie you are so lucky you did not sustain another blow. We are very careful to educate our patients that after a serious TBI, one cannot hit their head again for the first 12 months. Sallie answered defensively, "But I do ride with my helmet." The doctor calmly said to her, "Sallie, not even with a helmet. Not in a car accident. Not in any form. You are very lucky you did not sustain another blow to the head this past year. The brain can only take so many blows. I want you to know this, so you can be very careful." Sallie sat back in her chair, silent as she was trying to take it all in.

"That said, Sallie, clearly you have ridden yourself well." Sallie asked, "Why am I still struggling?" The Dr. went on to explain, "With a TBI of this magnitude, recovery, Sallie, is years long, possibly a life time. It takes thousands of repetitions for the brain to rewire." Still trying to take it all in, she asked, "Why am I worse now than 2009? I have gone backwards, it seems. I mean, swallowing for God's sakes, Who has this much trouble swallowing?" The doctor stared at her. "Often Sallie, we see neurological regression. Everyone is different. No two people's lives are the same. How much one regresses usually depends on what the home environment is like, and of course stress. Your home life appears to be quite good." Again, she sat silently trying to process what she was hearing. The doctor went on, "You've had a neuro psych evaluation. I am looking over the findings. You are mentally sound. You have no mental illness. Your IQ has been impacted. It's apparent, reading the results, you have real difficulty with focus and concentration. My recommendation is for you to receive speech therapy for the swallowing and occupational therapy for the cognitive damage. Again, you can regain some ground, but you must be allowed to make mistakes in doing small simple tasks, repetitively being allowed to make mistakes." The tears welled up in Sallies eyes as she said, "I don't have time for therapy. I have to work! We are going to lose everything we own, I have to work."

The doctor kindly and compassionately sat back in his chair took a deep breath and answered, "Sallie, with the issues you are suffering work is not an option. I don't believe I would recommend you go back to work. This was a very serious injury. Your efforts to come back this far are remarkable. But you must have occupational and speech therapy. Swallowing is essential to living." The doctor quickly asked, "By the way, you drove here correct?" Sallie nodded as she answered, "Yes." The doctor asked, "Who taught you to drive again? With this injury you clearly had to be taught." She nodded, "Yes. I had to be taught. My husband, he taught me. "The doctor looking at her nearly sternly asked, "and what credentials does your husband have to teach you to drive?" Sallie answered, "He's a police officer. A word of advice; don't ever have your husband who is a police officer teach you to drive." The doctor laughed and said, "It is hard for husbands and wives to teach each other." Sallie blurted, "Yes, especially if they are a police officer who believes in following every rule and law there ever was." The doctor smiled and said, "Well clearly he taught you thoroughly. I bet last year was a difficult year for your family with all the loss of Law Enforcement." Sallie nodded and replied, "It was."

The doctor continued on; "Stress Sallie, is the enemy after a TBI. Stress in general is not good. But after a TBI, stress can really cause issues with how the brain functions. This could be the reason for the regression. My heart goes out to you. You have battled through this, like a soldier." She sat in bewilderment as she nodded her head in agreement and some glimpse of understanding. She finally had what seemed to be an answer. Not the one she wanted. But at least she had understanding. It was not that she was not trying in life. Or had some overnight mental illness show up. She had sustained an injury to her brain.

The doctor pulled up her MRI on his computer. "This is your brain Sallie. Do you see all these white spots?" She could clearly see them, there were too many too count. "That is the scar. You bled significantly here. This is the front temporal region. "He then pulled up another image of her brain, "Do you see this region here?" as he pointed to the image. " This is a scar around the tentorial notch, from which your brain stem, major arteries and all cranial nerves travel to your brain and body." He pulled up one more area, "You might not see this as clearly. This is another angle. This is called the Ambient Cistern. You took a very significant blow here. The fact you drove here and walked in my office is impressive. The fact you speak so well is also impressive. Injuries to these areas create vision issues, swallowing issues, focus and concentration issues, and of course, severe physical pain. Due to these injuries, changes in weather and stress will often be triggers to disorientation, and exacerbate the issues these damaged nerves already present.

The appointment was over. As Sallie got up to leave she reached to shake the doctor's hand as she said, "Thank you." Much to her surprise, the doctor gave her a hug. "You have done simply an amazing job with your efforts to recover. Time is an asset and effort must be appreciated in your situation. You take care."

This new knowledge that she had sustained a traumatic brain injury helped Sallie make sense of the past two years. She had physical and cognitive deficits, including sensitivity to light and impairment of peripheral vision and depth perception. She didn't know why, but somehow riding Esco helped her neurons and axons in her brain rewire. She felt, somehow, relieved that she wasn't mentally insane, and that all of the over stimulation she had experienced driving and going into stores were real, and caused by her injury. She also, with this new information, felt tremendous compassion for Michael and Chayce, who obviously were helping her all that time in ways she had not been aware.

Sallie tried to digest all of the new knowledge. It would take months, years, to process all of the information. In the meantime, she would learn to function as a mentally stable person in a body that would throw curves at her all the time. One minute, it would be vertigo, the next it would be peripheral vision which was non-existent, legs she couldn't feel which she counted on to cue Esco, or hands that would tremor wildly while she was trying to drive, or trying to direct her horse. She couldn't control swallowing due to the nerve damage, so eating was a constant struggle. And sheer exhaustion with each effort to get better was heavily weighing on her. The neurologist had been clear. What wires together, fires together in the brain. It takes 10,000 repetitions to reconnect after a TBI. It's worse than being a baby with clear neuropathways to develop. With the damage she had sustained, the neurons and axons had to literally create new pathways around the damage to allow her body to function as it had before.

Sallie continued riding at home and had been for some time. Lessons were financially out of the question, but riding at home with no instruction wasn't enough to make her better. She had to have instruction and the guidance of her coach. "You must be asked to do small simple tasks repetitively," being allowed to make mistakes" are the words the neurologist used, and it was finally making sense to her and Michael as to why riding lessons had helped her so much.

Although Michael worried about their finances, he had come to realize how important lessons were to Sallie's rehabilitation, so he did what he could do and bought her one as a gift. A single lesson wouldn't be enough. Unless she did a certain activity every day, it was as if she had never done that activity before. The struggle had, so far, been long, nearly two years. It was a world of " try and try' again. If she didn't drive the horse trailer regularly, it was as if she had never driven one. If she did not drive a vehicle every day, when she got behind the driver's seat, it was all new to her. By the time she got to Osinski's facility, she'd be drenched in sweat— and she still had to face getting on Esco. She was having to rehab daily, but the lessons were not there daily. And the terrors were transferring to Esco's back, as well.

CHAPTER 12
OVERWHELMED

On his practical side, Michael had serious concerns. While he feared that they would lose everything they owned, it was just as hard to hear Sallie say she couldn't drive the horse trailer and that she needed a smaller one. He couldn't conceive of buying a new horse trailer, and Sallie, desperate to heal, couldn't understand the dire situation presented by their bills. In the past, it had been Sallie who took charge of their finances, and Michael who wrote out the checks and mailed them. As a commercial lender for years, Sallie knew how money worked, how businesses worked, and how cash flow went. She had spent 15 years building businesses, writing proposals and business plans, and working with private investors. She had built a strong financial background and had had the excellent credit score to evidence her success. But for two years, the bills had been left for Michael to sort out alone.

Sallie had asked to see the bills several times in the past year. Michael, not wanting to worry her, always had an excuse. Finally, he spread them out in front of her. She could only murmur, "We're done. We have to file bankruptcy." The numbers showed that they were in financial ruin and were likely to lose their farm. Sallie thought they'd have to sell their horses including Esco. Her body went cold, she felt responsible for this in every single way imaginable. "We're not filing bankruptcy," Michael said. "Michael, I would have to get a job for $2 million a year to pay this off," Sallie said. "We are filing bankruptcy." "No." he replied, as if the refusal would somehow change the facts.

Sallie was careful not to blame anyone for their financial troubles. She knew that the Great Recession had taken its toll on many across the country. She also knew had she never had the accident, it would not have beaten them down this far financially. Michael and Sallie had had a savings account before the accident. They were careful with money.

Sallie looked at Michael and said, "Did you get on a horse without a helmet?" Michael answered, "No."

"That's right, I did" Sallie answered. "Did you crash the world economy?"

"No." he replied.

Did you increase oil to 130 bucks a barrel?"

Once again, he said "No."

"That's right, you didn't," she said. "It is you and I against the world right now. And you and I are filing bankruptcy. That's what we're doing." Michael simply replied by saying "no". The idea of filing bankruptcy felt like castration to each of them. They had worked very hard over the years to pay bills and had maintained excellent credit scores, which dictated everything from how much you pay for insurance, to how employers viewed you. From Sallie's perspective life it seemed, was a credit score. Between getting the news she had had a life changing injury, and required speech and occupational therapy, and having to file bankruptcy for which she felt 100% responsible, Sallie, was devastated. Not only was she devastated, but while Michael was more stressed than she had ever seen him, he was still not ready to give up. He believed that if they could work their way through this period together, it would represent another victory for Sallie. It was a risk but one he felt necessary to take.

Before her injury, she enjoyed learning new things and did it easily. She was very disciplined and could push herself when needed to learn things quickly and thoroughly. She could hear a new phone number and dial it immediately and remember the phone number for ever . She had nearly a photographic memory. All of that was gone. In the two years following the accident, she had experienced how difficult it was to learn something new, such as the training modules at the bank and the paperwork to set up the nonprofit. She and Michael and Chayce witnessed what was progress in her recovery, only to watch it slip away.

After the discussion of bankruptcy with Michael, Sallie did what she knew she needed to do. She put together photos of her horses. And she posted sales ads for them on Facebook. Making the sales brochure for Esco caused her to physically shake. As she looked at each photo, tears streamed down her face. "Thank you Esco you gave me back, my sons" she thought as she watched a video clip. "You gave me back my husband Michael, Esco". Her hands trembled, and the waterfall of tears poured from her soul as she managed to put the information for his sale together. All of her horses were now posted for sale on Facebook. As she posted each ad, she had to walk away from the computer. Comments of 'friends' were coming in; "WHAT?" they would ask. Unable to cope any longer, she finally took a Xanax so she could continue with posting the final ad. It read " For Sale : EscogidoXXV~ The Chosen". She stared at the link in the status bar, for a few seconds…then pushed the button, "Post". Hearts can break, but Sallie actually felt hers shatter. She rose up from her computer chair feeling numb, then laid down for a nap.

It was later that day when Michael woke her up. "You put the horses for sale?" he asked quietly and calmly. It took Sallie a few moments to respond, "Yes." Michael sat in silence and was careful and deliberate in choosing his words, "It's not your fault babe." Sallie looked at him, "Yes it is. They are all listed now". Michael said, "I know people we are friends with are calling me asking if we are ok". Sallie replied by saying "Well, I am responsible, and I live up to my end of the bargain Michael. You know that." Both sat motionless, Sallie feeling shock, and Michael trying to imagine a way to unwind this tragedy. "I don't want you to sell Esco. I can now understand how much he is helping you. Don't sell him. Take him off the sales list." Michael said as he deeply exhaled. Sallie, feeling immersed in guilt answered, "He's just a horse. Logically he is just a horse. Never let your possession's own you, business 101" she replied in a defeated whisper. Both were sitting in a numbing silence when Michael's cell phone rang,

"Oh great, another call." he said. "Sallie, take him off. This is ridiculous."

"No, what is ridiculous is living life with this much struggle with an injury that was never explained from the get go, that's what is ridiculous." Sallie answered. "A life now of therapy? Where is that money going to come from? Being made to feel like I am a four barrel fuck up; being made to feel like such a loser. I told you riding made me better and no one listened, and you and grandpa, all of you people, could only say, 'Get a job!'. I have nothing to say Michael!"

Sallie had no tears left to cry. She had no answers to give. Every answer she found the past two years was either ignored or dismissed. "I am selling the horses. All I hear is how I have no job! I bring in no income! All I want to do is ride, like I am some little kid! This last year without riding lessons, all I have done is gotten worse, not better, and the only difference is I have taken, what, six lessons over the entire year of 2010? Esco, all he is doing is growing angry. His mind must be worked. He deserves to be in a place where an FEI rider can really work him. For the love of the horse, I am done. It's cruel to him for me to not know how to work him. And we need the money and cannot afford the expense. " Michael sat stoically, listening to Sallie's calm and reserved voice. He knew that to try and counter her argument in this moment, when she was feeling so defeated was futile. It was apparent to him that she was shutting down. Right before his eyes, she was throwing in the towel on life in general. She had no more fight left in her. She sat with a blank stare, a way he had never seen in her before.

Sallie's cell phone rang to break the silence. "G-r-r-eat" Sallie said under her breath as she answered the phone, "Yeah, Gramps." "Hey, I am in the area and I am going to stop by. Just making sure you were home. Is Michael there? " her grandfather asked. As she let out a deep sigh, she answered coldly, "yes." The usual dial tone was heard. Sallie had an unusual relationship with her grandfather. He was the family patriarch. Known and admired for his success in life, he was old school in his methods of teaching anyone anything. He was always observant. He would say outlandish things, and then step back to see what would happen and observe the reactions. He learned about people this way. He was known for holding people accountable and taking people to task. He was nearly always right when it came to making decisions. He had a keen sense of reading people, and he had learned along his life that most people needed to be pushed, as most gave up entirely too early. Sallie always remembered her grandfather telling her at a young age, "Sallie, you only have yourself to count on in life. Always remember that. "You only have you to count on, and as long as you understand that, you'll do fine". He was an antagonist if he was anything.

It was only moments after her phone rang that there was the knock at the door. "It's Gramps" Sallie said to Michael. She simply had no energy to move. She sat there on the couch still deep in thought trying to grasp the Neurologist appointment, how she needed therapy, how she had to sell horses and how much her life had really changed. Fear was something she never knew could be such an enemy.

She could overhear Michael and her grandfather exchanging greetings. Michael and her grandfather entered the living room. His presence was always felt long before it was seen. "Hi there" he said, right before he took a seat across from her. Sallie nodded; she was still paralyzed by her thoughts, trying to process all the neurologist had shared with her. Michael immediately went to the kitchen to bring out coffee along with crackers and a cheese plate for Sallie's grandfather. Sallie's Grandfather had always been kind to her before. He was always all business, but he was kind to her in his gruff, antagonistic way. It is fair to say he was unaware, as most people, the problems presented by a traumatic brain injury. He didn't know much of Sallie and Michael's situation, and like to pit people against each other.

Sallie sat quiet and aloof in the presence of her grandfather who said, "So the horses are for sale. I heard." It was suddenly obvious why he had chosen to stop by. Sallie could give no response. Michael came from the kitchen with the plate of cheese and crackers and sat it on the coffee table in the living room. He looked at Sallie's grandfather and said, "Yes, she listed them all, even Esco". Sallie's grandfather was quiet but still powerful as he watched Sallie sit. "Sallie these are good crackers, I bet they are expensive. Why do you buy such expensive crackers?" In a week voice Sallie answered, "They are whole grain. They are good for Michael and Chayce." Michael, carrying cups of coffee, sat those on the coffee table. Sallie's jaw hurt too much to even attempt to chew. And her swallowing attempts would often leave her choking. She just did not have the energy to even try to eat. Her grandfather then took a slice of cheese, as he said, "What kind of cheese is this? It looks like really good cheese." Sallie said nothing. Michael, in an attempt to have Sallie engage in the conversation asked her, "Babe! What kind of cheese is this?" Sallie again just sat, trying to digest internally how she would ever be able to swallow again. Would it get better? How could it get better? Would she die from choking to death? Michael could see she was deep in thought, so he said to her grandfather, "It's something from Costco that's all I can tell you." Her grandfather answered, "I bet it is expensive." Then he took a sip of coffee and asked, "This is really good coffee. It's very smooth. I bet it's expensive. "Michael immediately answered, "Actually it's not. It's from Costco, and Sallie has low blood sugar. For some reason this coffee doesn't seem to bother her." Her grandfather looked at Sallie and said, "If you would eat, you wouldn't have to buy such expensive coffee. What are you trying for anorexia?"

Sallie leaned her head back as she rolled her neck, and look at her grandfather, "My jaw. It's in a lot of pain. And I have this swallowing issue." Her grandfather cut her off, "When did all that start?" Sallie could not answer; she could not believe she would have to answer this question. Michael spoke for her, "The accident." Her grandfather then said, "Its best you sell those horses." Everyone was silent for a moment. Her grandfather, still staring at her said, "My god Sallie, with so many issues you have now, why don't you just shoot yourself and put Michael and Chayce out of their misery?" Michael politely laughed, hoping it might break the tension. Then he answered, 'No, we are not ready for her to leave. Chayce and I still need her." Perhaps it was because Michael's anger was starting to show in his face, but the comment signaled the end of the visit. Sallie's grandfather decided he needed to get going. Michael walked him to retrieve his coat. As Sallie sat there on the couch, she thought, "Why don't you just shoot yourself and put Michael and Chayce out of their misery" That did not sound like a bad idea to her. The Life insurance she had would significantly help the financial situation. It was pretty clear she would not have a career again. The amount of physical pain she was in daily was wearing her down. And her inability to swallow without choking was making it exhausting to even want to try to eat. After he left, she was even more exhausted. She was exhausted all the time. In between trying to eat and failing, she would sleep. She was withdrawing from everything and everyone even Esco.

Michael and Sallie continued to discuss bankruptcy as the weeks went on, but Michael flatly refused to consider it. Sallie kept the horses listed and looked for anything she could sell that had any value to attempt to help their spiraling finances. Michael knew Sallie needed speech therapy to help her with swallowing. The new found impact brought on by this emerging injury was adding yet stress and drain on him. Now he had to be present when she ate in order to help her during her choking episodes. "Just make the appointment for the speech therapy "Michael said. "We can't afford the gas to get there." Sallie answered. And it was true they had zero money. Michael's income was barely enough to cover the mortgage, much less food, hay, gas. The doctors had all suggested disability to her and two helped her file. The wait would be two years for disability she had paid into her entire working career. In the mean time, it was clear if they did not file bankruptcy, they would lose the farm.

Sallie was sobbing when she made the call. "Grandpa, I have gone to the doctor," she began. "Oh? Why?" he said. "You've gone to the doctor, huh?" "Yes, and they say I have these deficits from the accident with that horse, and that it's lifelong." "They do, huh?"
"Yeah, and I need rehab, and we can't afford it, because we are going to lose everything we own, and I just need a job." She paused to take a breath. "Can I just sweep out the shop?" There was a brief pause of silence. Her

grandfather said "Rehab? For what?" Sallie answered, "Occupational therapy, they said, and speech therapy to help me swallow." "The doctor is wrong Sallie. Nothing's wrong with your swallowing, It's all in your head. Did any of them tell you that?" Sallie retreated into a stunned silence. She had no courage or will left to argue with him. He was a man whose mind would not be changed once set. "Did you read the doctors report? I sent it to you." she quietly asked. "They are wrong. Sallie. Doctors are not always right" he said. Sallie had nothing to say. What could she say? Doctors can be wrong. She could not argue that.

Sallie's grandfather grew quiet. Then he said, "Send me all your bills. You send me all your bills. And you tell Michael not to be shy and give me Michael's number." Her grandfather made a call to Michael, who sent over the bills, all of them. To Sallie's relief, her grandfather soon called her back. "Yeah, Hey, I could send you all the money in the world. I could pay off your farm 10 times over!. But what good would that do?" he said. "You think you need this therapy, but there is nothing wrong with you. You had a job with the bank. You apparently did not like it, and quit. And that's your problem. You should have never left that job. You keep saying you have this or that or the other since that horse accident. There is nothing wrong with you. Maybe you and Michael and Chayce really need to live underneath a bridge, so you can see how it really is, because you wouldn't continue working. You did this to your family. You need to take responsibility for it. I am going to send enough money for you to file bankruptcy. That is what you both need to do. Sallie, you are my biggest disappointment."

Speechless, Sallie tightened her grip on the phone. She heard a click as he hung up. It was clear to her, it was all over. She looked at Michael, "He won't give me a job, I guess because I am not worth saving." as she looked across the farm through the living room window with a numbness in her soul. "We will file bankruptcy. Stop paying everything. Here is the number to the Attorney." She gave Michael the number as she passed him and began slowly walking up the stairs to her bedroom. For Michael, there was no sense, he recognized, in trying to counter her demand. It was apparent that the person lecturing him could no longer see the light of day. However, he felt an intense anger welling in his chest, a combination of frustration borne from indifferent doctors and misdiagnoses, as well as the on-going cascade of injuries, each one seemingly more severe than the previous. Then there was the calloused indifference he'd witnessed when Sallie's grandfather spoke to her. He pondered just how much more of this the family could take, knowing that they were still a long way from the end of this journey. The one thing, possibly the only thing he still felt certain about though, was that he loved Sallie and the boys, and he was not going to let their family come apart.

That wasn't the end of the matter. Her grandfather called again, and again, over the next few weeks, to tell Sallie that she needed to get a job, and those conversations fed into the guilt she was already carrying. Sallie thought her fears were easier to overcome than the oppressive guilt. Like the rest of the family, he understood little about traumatic brain injuries, and Sallie couldn't explain. All she knew was that she kept discovering new problems, and that doing well one week did not mean that she would do well the next.

Facing bankruptcy was defeating enough. Accepting her new self was a work in progress. Knowing her IQ had dropped was disappointing and depressing. Still, the family was slowly adjusting to Sallie's limitations. She could keep going if she had riding lessons, if she could keep riding Esco and learning. But now lessons were out of the question.

Her accident had caused this. She had done something wrong. She needed rehab, but there was no help for her. Riding lessons with Osinski were her only help. Riding Esco with instruction was exactly what had kept her challenging her issues. Lessons with Osinski were also rebuilding a stronger neurological network in her brain. Being given instructions, and having to execute them immediately, was her cognitive and occupational rehab long before she even knew what cognitive functions were, or what occupational therapy was. And it had been six months since her last lesson. She felt like a huge burden to everybody, and she lived in a state of tremendous guilt for the entire trauma she was creating for her family.

She didn't want to walk out the front door, go anywhere, or do anything. Michael had told her not to turn on the truck because there was no money. So driving, when she did drive, was a nightmare, because each time, about once a month, it was like learning how to drive all over again. It was overwhelming. The doctor had even told her, with her injury she had to practice each skill every day, and because of their finances, this was not possible. She had very much regressed in her recovery. Everything was a fight, even getting out of bed, or walking down the stairs. She would hear in her mind, "You cannot hit your head again." Swallowing, which was merely just choking, was too exhausting to even attempt. Not only was Sallie exhausted from the injury, so were Michael and Chayce.

In the past two years she had fallen several times because of her lack of coordination and inability to feel her left leg. She had already cost her family a great deal of heartache from hitting her head one time. If she fell down the stairs and hit her head again, where would that leave them then? The web of fear was weaving a wicked strong hold on her life. She felt like fragile glass, and sank into dark depression. It seemed that everything had turned to' no'. No help, no skill practice, no lessons, no, no, no! It was mentally exhausting. She wanted help, she wanted to get better. And everywhere she turned, the answer was, "No". It was as if lights were slowly dimming all around her. Animals pick up easily on the moods and emotions of the people they love, and Esco on nearly every ride in the last six months, also was also feeling her heavy weight of guilt and intense frustration. Esco was to the point that he did not even want her on his back.

Sallie felt rejection from everyone. Her husband, her grandfather, her sons, her entire family. Her friends had disappeared. Most were still unaware of the circumstances, but Sallie had grown out of touch, limited by finances and her personal disabilities. And the last nail in the coffin came when her own horse rejected her. She had finally been tested, and now felt confident, that she had never been diagnosed correctly after two long, hard years of fighting to be better. Finally, she could share this diagnosis with those who she was close with, but there was zero understanding. No one understood how life changing such an injury really was. And the lights just kept getting dimmer, and the walls closed in around her.

2011

CHAPTER 13
TIMING IS EVERYTHING

It was a cold March morning in 2011, when Michael went out fishing. Chayce was staying the weekend at a friend's house so Sallie awoke to an empty house. As she lay awake in bed, she glanced out the large bedroom windows overlooking the barn and the arena. The sky was a misty, foggy, a typical northwest winter day. She slowly got up, went to the bathroom. She looked into the mirror, hearing the words in her head, "You are my biggest disappointment." As she stared at the face in the mirror, she saw someone who had no future. The woman who looked back at her was pale, eyes sunken and dark, her cheeks, gaunt. Sallie reached down to the cupboard under the bathroom sink and went through the bathroom towels. She found two that were large. Used, but not in too good of shape. She walked back to her bed, laid both towels out across the top of her bed. She went to the top drawer of Michael's night stand, where he stored his gun. She opened the drawer. There it was Michael's gun. She stared at it for a moment, then reached down and removed the gun from its holster. She placed it on top of the night stand, emptily staring at its hard, blue, steel form. Almost instinctively, her hand reached out and picked it up once more. As she took the safety off, she heard her grandfather's words echo through her head, "My god! Why don't you just shoot yourself and put Michael and Chayce out of their misery? " "Perhaps he is right" she thought. She already felt dumber than her kids, and her new found IQ proved that she was. She already felt like she was only half the wife she used to be to Michael, recognizing how much he did and the struggle the last two years was for him. She wallowed in the misery she brought on her family; having to file bankruptcy because of the burden that she had become to her family. Needing rehabilitation therapy was financially out of the question and. the isolation she constantly felt was overwhelming. Tears freely rolled down her cheeks. She loved her kids and Michael, and she and felt confident that the life insurance would make things better for them than what she could offer as a wife and mother.

So there it was. Not taking her own life would only be another selfish act bringing more pain to the family she loved. All the testing confirmed there was long term permanent brain damage. She had wanted to be better and was willing to do anything to get better. But there could be no promise that it would happen, and there was no one to explain what better looked like. She was trapped in a world that was a web, a web of ignorance from which she seemed unable to escape. No one seemed to understand what a traumatic brain injury was, how debilitating, permanently, it could be. She marveled at the void her life had become. As she reached for the gun to rid everyone from her inability to pull her weight in society, her cell phone rang. The words, "Mike Osinski" flashed across the screen of her phone. If the noise of the phone had startled her, seeing the name, "Mike Osinski" startled her even more. Osinski had been her lifeline in every sense of the word. So without so much as a pause, she reached out to answer the phone.

Some may credit God's hand, others might say it was simply fate or karma; whatever the cause it was an intervention. "I haven't seen you in a while" came the voice from within the earpiece. It was the voice Sallie had heard floating through her headphones countless times. Mike Osinski was a coach for serious riders, and Sallie assumed that because she had taken only six lessons in the prior twelve months, he had taken on other students in her place. He was not a person who would call students, let alone her!

"How are you?" Osinski asked. "I'm fine," she murmured heavily. Almost unconsciously, she had carefully laid the gun back down on the night stand. "Sorry, Mike, I haven't been able to come to a lesson because we don't have any money." She heard a calm breath on the other end of the line, and then the soothing voice again. "Well, I need to see you and Esco. Bring me your horse." "No, really, Mike, I mean it. I don't mean we don't have money to go to Hawaii. I mean, I don't know how we're going to eat." "I didn't ask you for money," Osinski said., "I asked you to bring me your horse. I need to see you and Esco."

In that moment Sallie's head was full of Michael's voice: "I mean it, do not even turn on that truck. Every time you do, it costs us money." For the past six months, Sallie hadn't left the house, not even to go to the grocery store. She did nothing, because she was in solitary confinement—her punishment for quitting a job and not obtaining a new one. She had firmly believed that for months. "I can't drive down there, Mike." "You can." he said. "Do you have enough gas to get here?" "I do, but I don't know how I'm going to get home." "Bring me your horse, and if you need money to get home, I will see that you get it. Bring him down." he said, calmly, yet firmly. "OK," Sallie said hazily. "Let me hook up the trailer, and we will be there." He replied, "See you soon." Sallie replied, "OK".

As she looked at the towels she had laid on the bed to catch the mess she would have left by shooting herself, she thought; does anyone listen to me anymore? Does anyone on this earth hear my words? Even Osinski hadn't heard. She didn't have any money. Nothing made sense. When she reached out to her family to ask for a simple job that could also provide her therapy, that turned into "Send me your bills," which turned into "Go live under a bridge." When she told Michael there was something wrong with her, he told her to get a job. Now she was trying to tell her trainer she was broke, and he didn't seem to hear that. He just told her she was supposed to bring in her horse.

She picked up the towels off the bed and laid them on the foot board. Like an automaton, she picked up the gun, put the safety back on, put the gun back in its holster, carried it down stairs and put it on top of the gun safe. As she was slipping her coat on to make her walk down to the her barn, she called Michael, her husband, on her cell phone. "Hi Babe" he answered. Sallie said, "Hey. I put your gun on top of the gun safe in the den. I need you to lock up all your guns. I don't have time to shoot myself today. Osinski called. He wants to see Esco." Michael could feel his frustration well up in his stomach and replied "How many times do I have to tell you...we DON'T have the money." Sallie answered back, "I don't think you heard me. He didn't ask me for any money. He asked to see Esco." Michael replied, "And shoot yourself? What are you talking about?" Sallie had no energy left to fight or discuss anything, let alone in detail. She responded stoically by saying, "I need to hook up the trailer. Get the guns out of the house as soon as you get home" and with that, she hung up the phone. Michael heard the phone go dead, yet his brain was still trying to digest what he had just heard. His instinct told him that what Sallie had just confessed, that she had come close to taking her life, was not an exaggeration or fantasy. The tone of her voice, that deadpan tone, told him this was all very real. So that night he went home, rounded up all his firearms and ammunition, and went about storing it all within the gun safes or removing them from the house.

Exhausted, Sallie summoned the energy it took to hook up the heavy horse trailer. With little thought to the difficulty of movement, she got Esco out and loaded him into it. Driving the horse trailer was, as usual, a chore. Sallie could feel the smallest bump or Esco's tiniest movement. Not being able to swallow solid food and being on a near liquid diet had taken its toll. Her weight had dropped from the normal one hundred and thirty six, to only one hundred and twelve. Handling the heavy trailer down the highway felt like trying to control a roller coaster. She was shut down emotionally. She was oblivious to the road and the scenery. Nothing really mattered anymore. She drove slowly through the entrance to the barn, past the paddocks with fresh green grass just starting shoot through the dark earth. The drive just happened. Making the turn around the indoor riding arena, Sallie could see Osinski training his Grand Prix horse Pablo, a stunning black and white Pinto, in the arena. Sallie stopped to watch. Osinski and Pablo were working on tempi changes, upper-level dressage movements, and the coach was effortlessly dancing with the horse that was changing strides every two leads. "Well that is a sight few get to see." Sallie whispered to herself before driving on with the truck and trailer.

It took Sallie an enormous effort to park her rig and lead Esco out. The horse knew that Sallie was in a dark place. For the last several months, every ride in her home arena was a nightmare of PTSD flashes. Esco carried the weight of Sallie's soul upon his back. The weight was becoming too much for him to handle, as he would jump and spin in the air, doing a one-eighty turn with her on his back in protest. He had become angry. Esco knew where he was. He knew this was Osinski's place, the arena, where logic and reason rang. Esco had an unspoken faith in Osinski. Every time he ever saw this man, Esco's life was better. He trumpeted his return from the horse trailer.

Esco gave her a gentle look and nickered softly. As Sallie reached to untie Esco's lead rope, he nuzzled her arms. He stepped grandly out of the trailer, and Sallie sensed gentleness in him. He was trying to help her by standing still as she groomed and saddled him. When he saw the bridle, he lowered his head to pick the bit up out of Sallie's hand. He kept his head down, so Sallie could attach the lunge line easily. A physically weak, spiritually broken and emotionally shattered Sallie, lead Esco into the arena. "Good morning! How are you?" Osinski asked. Sallie forced a smile. "Good. Pablo looks great!" she quietly said.

She began to work with Esco on the lunge line. Kind and gentle with Sallie minutes before, it was as if Esco saw his chance to let Osinski know not all was well. Esco turned into a maniac on the end of the line, bouncing, bucking, and snorting. He raced around until he nearly fell over. If Sallie wasn't going to be honest with how bad her life was, surely Esco would not lie. Osinski frowned at Esco's wild behavior. "You cannot allow him to do that, Sallie. He's going to hurt himself." Sallie tried soothing cues and soft voice commands, but they were of little leadership or comfort to Esco. Osinski said, "Bump him in the mouth with that bit. Tell him that is not acceptable." With her hand on the lunge line, Sallie bumped his mouth. Esco stopped immediately and gave her his full attention. His look said "What?" "Send him forward in the walk." Osinski instructed. Sallie did so, and Esco began bucking, snorting, and bouncing again. So she bumped him a second time, which gave Esco comfort as he was not having to be the leader. Esco settled down, but when Sallie reversed direction on the lunge line, he started his antics once more.

It took half an hour before he was calm enough that Sallie could take him to the mounting block. She took a few deep breaths." Well, I was going to shoot myself today anyway. So, here it goes!" she muttered to herself. She swung her leg over Esco's back, and they walked a few laps in the arena. Sallie's mind began churning. She could hear the things people said to her. "You can't be that hurt if you still ride Esco." "For God's sake, you are having financial problems—yet you have an expensive horse!" "If you really cared about your family, you would sell that horse and save your family money. But you're just too selfish to do what is right for your husband and son."

Sallie felt tears come, and she closed her eyes for a moment. When she opened them, she happened to glance outside. A beautiful field unfolded at the bottom of a gentle sloping hill. She knew there was a trail among the trees, and it dawned on her that she had never taken Esco there. In fact she had never taken Esco, ever, out on the trail. Today seemed like a good day to go. Sallie felt a tiny glimmer of joy that led her to direct Esco to the trail head and onto the path. She just left the arena on Esco's back. As they rode away from anyone's sight, Sallie felt a tiny sense of freedom. For the first time ever since the accident, she was riding without someone either right next to the arena, or standing in the middle of an arena.

She had Esco walk down the hill into the meadow and onto the trail. The air was crisp, and the buds on the trees were starting to bloom forth in a multitude of feathery green shoots of leaves becoming. Esco seemed fascinated by the new sights, sounds, and smells on the trail. They passed a peacock farm, where Esco looked curiously at the colorful birds. They walked up a hill on the trail. And for the first time in months, Esco took a deep breath—and relaxed. In that quiet place, Sallie felt her turbulent spirit calm. She had forgotten how healing nature was to her, and how peaceful she felt among the trees. She and Esco had the beautiful place all to themselves. As she and Esco crested another hill, she could see the beautiful moss on the white trees, creating a beautiful contrast. She had forgotten the inner peace nature could provide. The rich deep green moss that grew across the forest floor created a view was spectacular to her.

A glimmer of joy welled up within her chest. It was just a whisper underneath the guilty echoes that came to mind. All she wanted to do was get better. She needed occupational therapy. She needed to be allowed to be given small, simple tasks in repetitive intervals and allowed to make mistakes. But for her, for some reason, no one in her circle seemed to understand. That was how a brain that has been injured could be healed. That was what doctors told her.

In the quiet, Sallie could hear the leaves from the previous winter crunch under Esco's hooves. The trail ride calmed her. She was by herself with her horse for the first time since the accident. The thought came to her like a memory: "This is where I belong." She had known it always, but in the peaceful moment, she could feel it in her soul.

As the trail looped around, bringing Sallie and Esco back to the barn, Sallie found she was smiling. She rode Esco back into the covered arena, where Osinski was riding another of his horses, George. "I took Esco on the trail for the first time ever," Sallie told him proudly. "And I rode all by myself! I haven't done that since the accident." "And he was a good boy?" Osinski nodded at Esco. "Yes, he was a saint!"

Osinski laughed. "Come on, then! Let's go again." He signaled for Sallie and Esco to follow him and his horse George to the trail. As they rode, Osinski talked about his upcoming shows. He asked Sallie how things were at home. She told him that she and Michael were filing bankruptcy and about how much she missed taking lessons, and not just because she loved Esco. "Riding him makes me better," she said. "There's something about riding and lessons that makes me better. You've seen it. I get better. The horse makes me better."

Sallie could see Osinski's profile, and he was nodding his head. Sallie didn't share the testing, or the results, with Osinski. He was unaware of the extent of the damage she had acquired. She feared his rejection, that he might tell her he couldn't work with her. He knew she was struggling, but not how much. "I'm a person who needs to achieve," she said choking back the tears. Sallie continued. "All I'm doing right now is failing in every area of my life." Her instructor was silent until they reached the last leg of the trail. The sky was a brilliant blue, and under it, birds were flying and chirping. Sallie's lips began to quiver. "Osinski, this isn't some little-girl fantasy," she said. "I'm a herd creature, and I need people, and I don't have a career anymore, so I see no one. I do nothing." "People are herd creatures," Osinski said, as George and Esco passed under an archway of branches. "We do need interaction with other people." Wiping away a flood of tears from her cheeks, Sallie said "Lessons are way for me to have goals and work toward them, to try to achieve something somewhere in my life. Right now, all I do is fail in every single area". Osinski nodded again. They had nearly completed the entire loop of the trail, and the barn was coming into view. He turned toward Sallie and gave her a thumbs-up. She understood the wordless message: "I get it. I get what you're saying, Sallie."

It really was a lovely day she thought as she drove home, one she would have missed had he not called. Once back at the house, Sallie put Esco away, then returned to the house to rest. Despite being alone, the thought of suicide that had gripped her earlier in the day was now gone. Michael was still at work, bound by a schedule that kept him there until midnight each day. Despite his absence, despite her inability to share with any other person the wild swing of emotions she had experienced in the past 12 hours, she was content to close her eyes and drift off to sleep…and she did.

CHAPTER 14
TAKES COURAGE TO RISE UP AND LIVE A LIFE

At home the rides on Esco were truly becoming dangerous for Sallie. Esco had absolutely had enough of being a therapy horse. He was simply tired of walking and trotting in circles, and he was becoming angry when she would ride him as she was that moment, having PTSD "flashes". Esco did not know how to handle her flashes. He would protest against Sallie under saddle. With each protest, Esco gained ground for leadership that Sallie had been loosing for the last 12 months with very few lessons. By mid-April, 2011, Esco had truly taken over leadership in the relationship. It was spring, and he was flexing his muscles each and every ride for Sallie. Physically, Sallie was losing weight rapidly due to her painful jaw, which was only getting worse. Sallie knew she could no longer ride Esco. She had to sell him. She sent Osinski an email, "I need you to sell him. I cannot ride him anymore." Osinski sent an email back, "Not until you work through your issues with him." Sallie sent an email back, "He won't even let me on his back. He is angry. And I physically do not have the strength or the ability to ride him."

Not only was Esco unwilling to carry Sallie, he was also bored. Over the last year with only six lessons for the entire year, Esco had had nothing to challenge his mind, and he began to bully Sallie and severely test his boundaries. His behavior broke Sallie's heart because her best friend would no longer allow her on his back, and he misbehaved every time she did manage to climb on. Osinski's email response was, "I need to see him. Bring him down tomorrow morning. Lesson is on me".

By this time Michael had come to realize that the riding lessons with Osinski were yielding some positive relief for his wife's injuries. Sallie had not said anything about it, believing that doing so would only add an additional burden to Michael's world. However, while he could not put his finger on the changes with any specificity, he recognized that with each lesson, her ability to function seemed to improve ever so slightly. The reality of taking lessons hadn't changed. He knew they did not have the money to pay for the gas to get to a lesson, let alone cover the cost of the lessons themselves. He chose to say nothing about his concerns for there was no denying that these lessons could be part of the answer to bringing Sallie back.

Sallie arrived for her next lesson, her jaw on fire with pain, her body frail after weeks of being unable to swallow food, but she managed a tight smile on her face to mask her pain. Osinski saw for himself how bad things had become. It was obvious in his observation that she was in no condition to handle Esco when he was behaving badly, and it would be dangerous for her to try until her physical strength and self-confidence improved. Osinski said to Sallie, "Here why don't I ride him for you today?" As Osinski took Esco, Sallie felt a tremendous sense of relief. Esco walked off with Osinski like a proud peacock. Osinski walked up to the mounting block. From observing Esco, he knew, he was in for a ride. Esco was prancing as if he was agitated. He snaked his neck, tossing it as if to say, "I am tired of carrying a bag of self-guilt, depression and a person who is terrified. I won't do it anymore! You can't make me!' Esco was expressing his own personal trauma. Osinski patted Esco's neck saying, "I know Esco, I know. Here we go." As he mounted, Esco exploded violently. Osinski had ridden this before, though he knew Esco knew better! The rearing and bucking took place for several minutes. This time Osinski could sense Esco was very upset indeed. Only he was bigger and more powerful. Osinski disciplined the horse, riding out the storm, commanding that his bucking and rearing was not acceptable in any form or fashion. After the explosive fight, Esco stood sweating and steaming. Finally, he licked and chewed, submitting to his rider. Osinski patted his neck while saying, "Your fine Esco, you're fine. Come on bud, let's work."

Osinski cued Esco to go right work, picking up the trot, and Esco seemed to happily perform. He did not offer to buck or rear at all for the rest of the ride. Sallie even heard Osinski giggle while riding Esco. She watched Esco's expression while Osinski was asking him to canter. Esco suddenly jumped 10 feet to the side, feeling freed! Osinski corrected Esco, and then asked him for the canter again. Esco again jumped 10 feet to the other side. Osinski corrected Esco, and he settled into the canter, but Osinski did not ride Esco straight down the long side of the arena this time. He asked Esco to move diagonally across the arena in the canter. As Osinski came closer to Sallie, he quietly said, "This is what we want in FEI. Right here. This is exactly what you want in canter half pass." And he quickly and gently patted Esco's neck.

Osinski was an accomplished rider. He had been to the Grand Prix too many times to count in his 30 plus year career. He knew how to ask for upper level movements. Vast in his knowledge and understanding of Dressage, he knew how to ride Esco. Much of what Esco offered Sallie was avoidance behavior. While the lay person might suspect that Esco was protesting Sallie's direction for him to work, the truth was that his resistance was rooted in his effort to fight the affect that Sallie's PTSD presented for both of them! Perhaps Osinski knew how to turn Esco's avoidance behavior into work. When the ride was finished, Osinski patted Esco saying, "Good boy!"

As he looked at Sallie, Osinski said, "He is smart. He's real smart. But we always knew that. He needs work Sallie." Osinski was riding Esco in the walk, cooling him out as Sallie said, "I know he needs work. But we are filing bankruptcy. I don't take lessons from you for any reason other than we honestly don't have the money." Esco had his head down, relaxed, walking, while Osinski was still cooling him out under saddle. Esco licked and chewed, his eyes flashing with a sense of pride and accomplishment. . Osinski was thinking as he again patted Esco. He asked Sallie, "When you listed him for sale on Facebook, did you catch any interest?" Sallie immediately said, "Oh, yes, after reading all the "O-M-G! You're WHAT?" Osinski nodded his head still quiet. "He deserves better, Sallie murmured. Esco deserves someone who knows the upper levels in Dressage. He is smart. He wants to do more than just walk and trot and canter a few strides on a 20 meter circle. And that is all I am able to do." Osinski looked at Sallie, this time catching her eye and asked, "What do you think or feel when you ride him?" Sallie was surprised. No one had ever asked what her thoughts were or how she felt about anything the past few years. "My heart, it can beat so hard in my chest, my chest, my heart it feels like it's going to jump out of my chest and fall out on the pommel of the saddle. My jaw, my jaw hurts so bad Osinski; sometimes it feels like it is going to fall off, it hurts so badly." Sallie said. "All I'm thinking is, don't fall, don't fall, oh God, please don't fall, with each and every single stride. I just beg; don't fall, please don't fall." Osinski's eyes widened. She had never mentioned this before.

"You need to be off Esco," he stated. "What is your schedule like during the week?" he asked. Sallie answered, "I have speech therapy twice a week. "She had finally just begun speech therapy to address the swallowing issues so she could eat. I have some doctors' appointments coming up. They found out I have a crushed disk in my jaw from when Esco fell on me. The doctors just figured out from another new MRI that my eye socket was broke, along with my cheek bone, but they say the disk that was crushed is what is causing a lot of pain because of the extensive nerve damage."

Osinski asked, "Could you haul him down here? I can ride him for you until I help you sell him, but I have to have him here." Sallie was surprised that he would listen to her concerns. It was the first time someone not only listened to her, but was willing to help her.   And he was important, a professional and well known! Osinski didn't laugh. There was no sarcasm. He didn't laugh or make jokes about her issues. He didn't tell her, "Get over it." He listened! Sallie was physically weak, and Osinski could see she was often rubbing her jaw. Internally he observed that she was shrinking physically. "I can haul him" Sallie said as she pondered her circumstances. Osinski looked at her and said, "Ok, you haul him in, and I will ride him for you and help you get him sold."

After a few weeks of hauling Esco three days a week to the training facility, in between her speech therapy and doctors' appointments, Osinski sent her a text message: "Someone has sponsored Esco's board for a month. Pack him up and move him here." Apparently a mutual friend had become aware of Sallie's plight and paid for Esco's keep for one month! Sallie was ecstatic, touched by the gesture and grateful. When Sallie and

Michael hauled Esco to the training center to move him in, Osinski could clearly see how weak Sallie was getting. She was out of breath and moved with effort. "Thank you Osinski for helping me. I feel so bad I can't pay you." Sallie said. "You just get better. We need you to get better Sallie." Osinski said to her. Come down and tack and groom for me on the days you can. But you need to get stronger.

Due to the pain her in jaw from what had finally been diagnosed as a crushed disk, Sallie had not been able to eat solid foods for the past two months. She had finally been sent to a maxio-facial doctor who examined her. He had immediately said, "You clearly broke bones in your face." The MRI confirmed that she had been living with severe damage no one had "noticed" before. She was very thin and frail. It was clear she was in tremendous pain. She had gone to meet with the surgeon over this period of time as well. After meeting with him, he had recommended a modified – condylotomy. He also told her the surgery would not be covered by her insurance company. She had to investigate if the surgery could be paid for as she was in so much pain, and often her jaw locked and popped. After calls to the Attorney General, and calls to the insurance company, she was at a dead end. She was in absolute agony, even taking 3600 mg of Ibuprofen a day for the prior few months. She could not continue in her condition. Her doctors had grown concerned with her loss of weight. By 2011 she had dropped to 112 pounds and was still losing. She was told her health was deteriorating with this steady weight loss. "No one can live in pain like this." She said to herself. "If modern western medicine can't help, maybe eastern medicine can". She had reached out in desperation to an acupuncturist. Surprisingly, the man got her in on an emergency basis on a Sunday.

With each session her jaw started to feel much better. After eight sessions, the pain became manageable. She was still going to speech therapy, and after two months, it also helped with her ability to eat solid foods. She had begun to make progress. This brought some relief to both Sallie and Michael. Osinski could also see that Sallie seemed to be getting better, and she was at the facility helping groom all four days. She could not stay for more than a couple of hours, but she was there, and she was making effort in grooming. Sallie was relieved that Esco was finally at full work with a rider who had balance, confidence, and leadership. As she began getting stronger, she was able to groom more for Osinski on a steady basis. She still had not been on a horse for a couple of months. While Osinski rode Esco, she groomed the horses; put on their saddles, and made sure they had the right equipment: blanket, saddle, and bridle. She struggled at first, often putting one horse's bridle or saddle on another horse. It was that annoying thing she was still doing confusing herself.

One day, Osinski would say, "All the saddles are on the wrong horses. Yesterday you tacked everyone just fine. I am trying to find the logic in this." "He was so calm and so cool, Sallie felt she could answer, "Brain Injury." Osinski looked at her and looked back at the horses He slowly drew in a calming breath and said, "Ok come here." He and Sallie took all the saddles off the horses. Osinski then went to the first horse in the cross tie aisle. "Which horse is this?" Sallie answered, "Falada." Osinski said, "Right. She is the grey horse who is white. She gets the black saddle because all dressage saddles are black. See the grey metal strip right here? This is a grey strip on the black saddle for the grey horse that is white. This is her saddle and always will be." Sallie fully understood that. "The grey horse that is white gets the black saddle with the grey metal strip on the back." He went to the next horse in the cross ties, "And who is this" Osinski asked again. "Prince" Sallie answered. "Yes, and Prince is a Chestnut with a white blaze and white legs. So Prince's saddle is the black saddle with brown piping"

Sallie fully understood, " Chestnut horse with a white blaze and white legs gets the black saddle with brown piping. Then Osinski went to the next horse in the cross ties, "Who is this?" Sallie smiled, "George, and he is chestnut too." Osinski laughed, "Yes, and because George is a chestnut with no markings at all. He gets the black saddle just a solid black saddle." That made perfect sense to her. Osinski had given Sallie a way she could remember. He did not make her feel smaller than she felt. He empowered her giving her cues so she would never again forget which saddle went on which horse. Sallie kept doing the same tasks over, and over, and over again, knowing it was the right thing to do. At the end of each day, Osinski would ask, "I'll see you tomorrow?" With a soft and gentle smile, she would answer, "Yes. I'll see you tomorrow." Those words were as healing as the repetitive tasks Sallie performed, and her confidence began to re-grow.

With Esco now in Osinski's barn, the trainer had gotten to know the horse well. Osinski had never had Esco in his barn before. It was Sallie who hauled him in and then hauled him out. One day, Osinski walked into the tack room and said to Sallie, "I want you to come out here." She followed him out to the arena. He got on Esco and rode in a circle around Sallie. "This is a good horse, Sallie," the trainer said. "He was confused, and there were some things he needed straightened out, but I straightened them out." Over the past weeks, Osinski had become impressed with the horse's work ethic as well as his talent. Esco was not Olympic team quality, but he could do well at FEI competitions. "I want you to give him another try. He is safe. He is sane. He is a great horse for you." Sallie stood in the arena thinking. She both loved and hated Esco. Her pain in her jaw was only just now starting to become manageable. She and her husband were filing bankruptcy, and they had sold everything they could. She still had other horses on the market they had never intended to sell, and still had not sold.. Cody was the big black horse Sallie had first ridden after the accident. But the economy was bad all across the USA.

Osinski seemed to know what she was thinking. "Financially, if you absolutely have to sell him, I get it," he told her. "But if it's that you're afraid, let me help you. Just grab my hand, and I'll help you through this. You're tacking and grooming for me, it is working. So, I don't mind training him for you." Sallie stood there watching Osinski ride Esco when she cleared her throat and said, "You will help me?" Osinski looked at her and nodded, "Yes I will help you." She decided she would rise up and follow Osinski's lead, because she truly loved her horse, and there was something about riding Esco specifically that did make her better. Physically and cognitively. Osinski had offered her a gift and she couldn't refuse it.

Osinski knew Sallie had not been on a horse for a while, and he needed to help her gain some sort of confidence of any kind. She was not just thin, she was more timid and broken than when they had first met, broken and beaten down by life. Their routine the past month had changed a bit. When Osinski was on the last of his horses, he would have her go get Esco. She would then lunge Esco, for 20 to 30 minutes allowing him to get his wiggles out while Osinski was riding his last horse. Osinski would then hand her the horse he had just finished riding, and say, "When you're done putting this horse away, don't worry about the tack, I want you to come watch while I work Esco". Osinski was schooling Esco and educating him to what was acceptable and unacceptable behavior under saddle. His rides on Esco were 30- 40 minutes. This is what it took for Esco, and this had been the routine for the past month.

It was good for Sallie to see someone riding Esco, to see that he could take discipline without being always being so defensive. Remembering the rides Sallie had had on Esco the past year with no instruction, she had nearly forgot that Esco could behave and was a joy to ride. She found herself doubting if she could overcome the PTSD flashes she had on Esco's back. Watching each ride Osinski made on Esco was proving to her Esco was good, but with Osinski's skills. She doubted her riding abilities. She doubted nearly all of her abilities. Osinski, finally asked Sallie, "How's your jaw today?" She nodded her head as she said, "Its better. Still hurts but better." Still on Esco, he said to Sallie, "I want you to try Esco today. He's been good." Osinski could see the hesitation in Sallie. "Go get your helmet, gloves and boots on. I'll be here waiting for you." he commanded. Sallie returned dressed to ride. He dismounted, walked Esco back to the mounting block and held him there.

Still frail and thin of frame, Sallie walked up the steps with zero trust or confidence. Osinski immediately went right into coaching mode." Shorten the rein" Osinski said to Sallie right at the mounting block. "He's safe to ride, but he will lead if you let him. So it's your job right now from the mounting block to show him you are the leader." Osinski would continue, "Get on. He wants to go. Sallie, with a horse like this you must just get right on with no stalling at the mounting block. Get on" he urged! She took a deep breath and quickly mounted Esco. Osinski immediately said "Good. Ok Sallie, right here on a 20 meter circle, right here around me. You just keep him on the bit and ask him to walk." As Sallie and Esco walked on a circle around Osinski, he could clearly see she was filled with self-doubt. Fear was in control and leadership was lacking on Sallie's part. Osinski knew Esco, and he knew he absolutely was a horse who would take over any chance he was given. "Sallie, take up contact. Shorten the rein. Come on, shorter." His voice was firm but encouraging. It would take several strides for Sallie to coordinate her fingers and hands to shorten the reins enough to make a noticeable difference. Once Osinski could see they were short enough, he continued coaching and said, "Ok good and now Sallie, rising trot." Within a few strides of trot, he would coach, "Come on ask him to reach more in the trot. He can cover more ground Sallie. I just rode him." Osinski saw little improvement in Esco's strides. "Come on Sallie. Come on!" he coaxed. With both legs, you encourage him. Ok, you have a whip. Reinforce your leg with a gentle tap of the whip. "As Esco's stride began to open up and cover more ground, Osinski immediately went into praising, "Good Job! Good for you Sallie. Just like that. You keep him moving forward just like that trot." Osinski saw Sallie's effort, but he also noticed it was a tremendous physical struggle. He was proud of Esco responding to her faint and slow cues.

It was clear to Osinski, a trainer and riding coach for over 30 years, that Sallie needed more time to execute an aide. She was slower in her reaction time than she had been in 2008 when he first started giving lessons. Osinski's perception was spot on. Sallie had neurologically regressed in the past year. She had hit bottom, physically and emotionally She was drained. He could see it. But here she was. And here he was, coaching her. He could see she was trying to rally when riding Esco. "Come on Sallie, send him more forward. He wants to work. He's ready to work." as Sallie still was struggling to get Esco to reach more with his legs and cover more ground in the trot. Osinski could see Esco wanting to start taking the leadership role as he was rooting with his neck more in the rein, trying to guess what Sallie was asking for. "Sallie, you must lead him. You must tap with both legs and reinforce with the whip and mean it. He is trying to understand what you want." Esco balked a bit with her leg aides. Osinski said, "Come on! He must respect your aides. You can't stop riding because he gets confused and stops. Be the leader this horse needs and deserves you to be!' Sallie again tapped with her legs, and reinforced with the whip, Esco seemed to now understand her aides would be different than Osinski's, but this was in fact the aide to move forward in the trot. "Good Sallie and you pat him. You let him know he is a good boy. And you keep him forward in the trot. If he backs off , you ask with both legs and reinforce with the whip. And you make sure you pat him. He must know when he is good and made the right choice." Sallie struggled to make her body work to produce the correct cues, to move him forward, to cantor, to react to right and left lead changes. The PTSD flashes would come and go as she fought to control him, and her left hand,   significantly weaker than her left was problematic. When she was fatigued, her left hand would tremor wildly. And the vertigo would come and go depending on the barometric pressure. Doing well on Esco would depend on regaining confidence and regaining fine motor skills that continued to evade her. Every ride was terrifying. And she was continually dropping out of the stirrups. But she pushed herself with every ride.

The sponsored month was almost up, which meant Sallie would have to take Esco home and begin the much dreaded hauling of the horse trailer back and forth to Osinski's barn. Osinski told her, "I don't know how Sallie, but I know it will work out where you get to keep Esco here. A horse will sell. Something will happen so you can keep him here." and it did. They sold one of their horses, and that would bring in enough money to pay her board for the next nine months. The sale of this horse was difficult for Michael, as he had raised the gelding since it was a foal. However, the sale also meant that the lessons and grooming with Esco could continue without interruption, and in this moment, that would be the priority for both Sallie and Michael.

2011 continued to evidence small improvements in Sallie's condition. Indeed, Michael had witnessed positive changes in her motor skills, her balance, and her memory. For Sallie, the routine of grooming and tacking had become something that provided her with motivation. Sallie would set her alarm clock every evening to ensure she would get up and get to the training facility on time the following day. She now had a purpose if nothing else. She took it as responsibility, and she took it seriously, as serious as she did with any career she previously had. Her drives to the facility were no longer filled with PTSD. There would be an occasional 'flash' but not nearly to the degree it was. The over stimulation she had been experiencing over the years seemed to be diminishing. Each drive, in itself, was a form of rehab therapy.

Each and every day she arrived to the training facility, she would be greeted with bright eyes of horses finishing their hay followed with the cheerful words, "Good morning!" from Osinski. Osinski would write down the horses in the order she was to tack and groom them. Esco was always worked last, so Osinski could be right there to instruct her. Sallie very much needed his reassurance. It was not like she was learning to drive again. A truck does not have a mind of its own. It cannot just accelerate on its own, someone must have their foot on the gas pedal. Sallie had to earn Esco's trust back, and Esco had to earn Sallie's. She had to step up and believe in herself, and Esco had to trust that Sallie did believe in herself.

Osinski had noticed she did have a serious issue with focus and concentration. In dealing with many different learning styles over the years, Osinski found that Sallie learned best in short 15-20 minutes lessons. He had to pick one thing and really coach her. This was the new routine. Short pointed lessons every day was what was working for her. At times her cognitive symptoms interfered. Sometimes in the middle of a lesson, she would lose focus and space out. At worst, she'd have one of her PTSD flashbacks, and at best, her mind would simply wander. When that happened, Sallie would soon hear Osinski's voice through her earphones.

"Sallie, hello, come back…" Sallie discovered that if she could turn her head and find him, she would know where she was again. He gave her mind a point of focus.

Back in the tack room, Sallie told Osinski that Esco felt "tippy" to her. Osinski addressed that in their next lesson, asking her to walk Esco the entire length of the 200-by-100-foot arena. To do this, Sallie would have to walk her horse far from her trainer, and she wasn't eager to leave Osinski's side. But he gave her courage. "The horses that can do FEI, they do feel tippy," he told her. "They're athletes, not big, wide draft horses. They bend and are supple. As I watch him walk, I can assure you he's putting each hoof perfectly flat on the ground. He's landing very balanced. So you don't need to worry about him falling." Sallie was listening and thinking. So many people had warned her not to ride again that she couldn't believe what she was hearing. "I want you to notice his stride," Osinski said. "I want you to feel how he feels under you. He does not take up all the space between your leg. I want you to feel it, feel this stride … this stride … and this stride." With his voice in her ears, Sallie found she could focus her awareness on her body and feel Esco's motion. "The last five strides do not matter, they are gone!" Osinski said. "The next 10 strides do not matter—they are not here. You ride this stride! This stride…and this stride." He turned to watch as Sallie and Esco circled the arena. "If a bird flew in and pecked him on the nose, it doesn't matter, you keep him going in this stride."

This stride … this stride … this stride … Osinski called out the words, and they resonated within Sallie's mind. From then on, whenever a flashback exploded in Sallie's mind, she would shake her head and remind herself internally, "You ride this stride! This stride, this stride, the next 10 do not matter." The words showed Sallie she had to get present in life. She took it to heart and began meditating at home daily. Meditating became part of her daily living routine, and it did not come easy to her. Making it a habit to set aside 30 minutes every day, faithfully, was easy. To practice meditation was a different story. To retrain her mind to just effortlessly be in focus in the moment became crucial. Focusing in the moment became her weapon against PTSD. Some people would want to choose the word 'tool'. But for Sallie, in no way was the word 'tool' a strong enough word. Meditation, focusing in the moment,   was her weapon to abolish PTSD. She had become sick to death of PTSD flashes. They had pinned her to the ground up until this point. She was now fighting a fight. With each and every ride on Esco she had to endure, she was now riding to the challenge to overcome PTSD flashes, which at times, left her feeling as though she were facing her executioner.

With each lesson, Sallie's anxiety diminished, if only a tiny bit. On many days she had something good to think about rather than the guilt and anxiety, the "demonic fear from hell." Riding Esco still felt like facing her executioner, but little by little, she was starting to trust him again, while replenishing the confidence she once had to an abundant level. "Shorten up your rein," Osinski told her in one lesson. "You keep dropping him."
In dressage, the rider keeps the reins short to maintain constant communication between the rider's hand and the bit in the horse's mouth. It had been difficult for Sallie to get the feel of Esco's mouth. She would allow the reins to lengthen until she was dropping Esco, or cutting off their means of communication.

Horses rely on the rider not to drop them, and it's hard on them to lose the rider's support. It was up to Osinski to explain what Esco needed from her in terms she could understand at that point in her recovery. "I want you to take both reins, just like you're holding the hand of two little boys, one in each hand remember? Like I told you back when you very first started riding with me." he said. "And I want you to have the conversation by holding their hands. You're going to feel Esco want to squirm out of your hands, and not wanting the contact, just like a little boy will do. They want to let go of their mama's hand and go running across the parking lot, but you know if you let them do that, they're going to get hit by a truck. You just calmly and quietly—with your hand communication—say 'No, you're going to hold your mama's hand'". Osinski taught her to behave like a parent when Esco acted up and refused to canter. "This is your son telling you he's not going to do the dishes," Osinski said, "and you tell him to get his butt in the kitchen and do the dishes. You tell Esco to get in canter. Tell him, Sallie. Don't let him walk all over you." Esco squirmed and pulled the reins. "Do not let him break the contact with your hand," Osinski said. "Tell him, by using your hands, to hang on and let you guide him."

When Sallie made the connection, her trainer saw it. "Good, he's on the bit and connected. Now, rising trot" Osinski commanded. "Sallie, keep the connection, do not let him give up the contact." When the rising trot was successful, Osinski instructed them to canter—and Sallie dropped the connection. Esco's movements looked sloppy, and Sallie seemed confused and unhappy. But Osinski was there to guide them. "Bring him back down to trot, get organized again, and canter again." Sallie tried again, and soon Esco was cantering. "Don't you quit! Keep him connected on the bit, and do not let that little boy let go of your hand. Move those legs of yours and keep him moving in the canter." But Sallie lost focus for a moment and was unable to move her legs. "If you do not move those legs, there is no need for me to waste my breath," Osinski urged her. "You move those legs in the canter, or I am going to leave the arena." With an effort—and some faith— Sallie willed her legs to move, and they did. Osinski nodded.

As Esco began to slow down, Osinski's voice floated through her headphones. "Sallie. You do not quit riding. Be the leader this horse needs and deserves you to be!"

The leader, Sallie thought. My life needs a leader. And that leader has to be me. The timing of that lesson was excellent. Chayce had moved into his teenage years, but he remembered that he was the one who had taught his mother to walk and speak again. In essence, their parent-child relationship was reversed. As Chayce got older and challenged his parents, as all teenagers do, Sallie struggled with him. As she took Esco by the reins and became a solid leader, she would begin again to take Chayce in hand and guide him when he needed it.

One day Osinski approached her with some news: a prospective buyer had inquired about Escogido. Sallie was hauling out tack for the horses when she stopped what she was doing. "OK," she said. "Well, I'd be an absolute fool not to take a look at it." "Exactly," Osinski said. A veterinarian arrived to examine Esco for the buyer. As part of the examination, he conducted a flexion test. He picked up Esco's legs, one by one, and tested their flexibility. During a flexion test, the vet will hold a horse's leg for 60 seconds, and then release it. As the horse walks away, the vet will look for signs of lameness. A healthy horse will move without stiffness or a change in stride.

During his test, Esco behaved as if his legs were broken. After the vet released one of his legs, he appeared ready to fall to the ground—not the typical reaction of a healthy horse. Flexion was graded on a scale of 0, meaning there is no sign of lameness, to 5, meaning the horse is lame. Esco's results were 3 on the front legs and 4 on the back. Sallie was shocked. According to the test results, her athletic horse was completely lame. She was furious for Esco was pulling one of his stunts again! She thanked the vet, then put Escogido in his cross ties and walked away, so angry at the horse that she couldn't speak. She wandered into the tack room, where she tried taking deep breaths to calm herself down.

She was still fuming when another rider found her, a bewildered look on her face. "Sallie, Esco looks like he's crying," the rider said. No one but Sallie and Osinski knew that Esco had been put up for sale. Though she was still angry, Sallie could picture Esco's eyes and posture. And she knew Esco needed her. "I'll be out in a minute," Sallie told the other rider. She took another deep breath, then walked out of the tack room. In the cross ties stood Escogido, head hanging low, a crushed and shattered look in his eyes. Sallie saw a tear streaming down the side of his nose, and knew the depth of Esco's sadness. She took him out of the cross ties and led him away. "If you want to stay with me, that's fine, but you have to be good," Sallie told him in a firm but quiet voice. "You have to behave every single day, and you can never be bad again, not ever! " Esco understood. He began licking and chewing contentedly as he followed Sallie back to his paddock. She removed his halter. She texted Osinski with the words "He failed." A message came back: "What do you mean, failed? What the hell?" When Sallie told him Esco had tested 3 and 4 in his front and back legs, Osinski was concerned.

"There is something going on. You need to get x-rays done," he said.

"Well, I told the vet I don't believe it," Sallie said.

Osinski laughed. "Sallie, you can't really fake a 3 and a 4."

"I still don't believe it. I am calling it bullshit, and I want him flexed again in 30 days."

"That's reasonable," Osinski said. "Do you feel anything wrong with him when you're riding him?"

"No, I don't feel anything."

Sallie's talk with Esco clearly reached the heart of the horse. Thirty days later, the vet came back and flexed Esco's legs again. Each time the vet released Esco, the horse was off like a shot. He was healthy and agile.

Sallie looked at the vet. "How is that possible?"

"Easy," he replied. "He just didn't want to be sold."

Sallie let out a puff of air. "Is that normal?"

"No, it's not normal, but it's Esco," the vet said, "and he doesn't seem to be normal."

When the Osinkski heard the news of the successful flexion test, he asked Sallie to make a decision about selling Esco as the buyer were still interested. Sallie thought about it as she stood with Esco in the arena. Osinski was riding another horse in a 20-meter circle around them. "I feel I owe you a commission," Sallie told him. "You've done so much for me. You've given me all these lessons." "You don't owe me anything," Osinski said. "I don't want you to think about me. This is for you. I want to know what you want to do." The decision was a tough one, and not only because it involved selling Esco. As Sallie made her recovery, she had asked her loved ones for help, and they had not been supportive nor understanding. This taught her not to ask for help, it taught her not to ask for anything. Sallie could hear their voices in her mind: "Sell that horse." "Is riding really so important to you that you would continue to ride that horse?" Her confidence had been shaken so badly by a few people that she had wondered if she was worthy to go on living. But on Esco with Osinkski's coaching she was building back her balance and confidence. She looked at Osinski and said, "I have to stay my course. I can't sell him, I would be selling a piece of my heart." Osinski immediately gave her a thumbs-up, then rode over to pat Esco. "Good for you. I think you're making the right decision. He's a great horse. And you're going to have a lot of fun with him and a long future with him."

174

They got back to work. Sallie focused on holding herself like a leader and conveying that to Esco through her hands and legs. Cantering had been tough for her, so she rode laps and laps in the canter with Esco, day after day. Osinski noticed her effort and improvement. He sometimes stood outside the arena by the gate, and as Sallie passed him, he would say, just loud enough for her to hear, "Canter is fun now, Sallie, yes?"

The late September day had been hot, and Mike Osinski and Sallie had worked through half of it. "Want to grab something to eat before your lesson?" Osinski asked Sallie. "Sure, that'll be great." At the restaurant, while waiting for their food to arrive, Sallie gave Osinski a searching look. "Why did you do it?" she blurted out. "Do what?" he asked. "Why did you bring me in, and take my horse on and train him, and let me be your working student? Why did you do it?" "Someone once reached out to me," he said. Although Osinski is now openly gay, during the first days after he came out, he was suicidal. He didn't know how his new life would work. He was very down. He told Sallie that someone had really helped him rediscover himself and was nurturing and motherly toward him. About a year later, Osinski felt he was on solid ground.

When he first met Sallie, he could feel a presence, a life force, around her as she began her dressage lessons. After her absence, when he had told her to come and bring Esco and not worry about money, he got a different impression. "When I saw you again, you had shrunk. And I was worried about you." Sallie smiled at him. "I've never been so happy in my life that you're gay." Osinski's eyes widened in surprise. "Happy? What? Why is that?" "Because you're a male, a strong male, and I needed that. You have the physical strength I don't have. Yet I'm happily married and truly married to my best friend, so no lines can ever get crossed, ever, so you're safe." He looked at Sallie and smiled. "Well, how about that?"

As they both ate, Sallie thought, "Finally, someone with compassion and absolutely no hidden agenda genuinely cares."

"OK," Osinski said, "we need to talk show season." Sallie listened as he outlined his plan. "We need to get you out there and competing," he said. "I'll take him out at first level dressage for you. I'll ride him first and help you get on him and get him warmed up, and then you will compete with him training level dressage." He gave her a serious look. "Do whatever you have to do. Sell whatever you have to sell, tack, brushes, anything. Sell it and start saving up your money for show season 2012." Oh my God, we already liquidated everything a year ago, Sallie thought. What am I going to sell now? She listened as Osinski continued. "There are a hundred mistakes that you have to make, and no one can help you with that," he said. "You have to learn on your own. Everyone has a way to get into their zone. Nobody can get you in that zone or tell you how to get in that zone, except for you." Sallie also shared her concerns with hauling a horse trailer on the freeway. "It's not that I am afraid to haul ", she said to Osinski. "My timing… for braking. If someone cut me off on the freeway, I am not sure I could react quickly enough to stop in time, with the weight of the trailer." Osinski listened as he thought about how he could see when she rode Esco that he also had to give her more time to give aides. "I understand Sallie. I will haul him for you to the shows. You just follow me in your car, and I will haul him."   That was great news for Sallie. She could drive; her coordination to drive was fully there. But, hauling the weight of the horse trailer on the freeway with her beloved Esco, she knew she was not yet quick enough in her reaction time.

Later that evening, Sallie turned to her friends on Facebook, telling them she was training for the 2012 show season but didn't know how she would pay the entrance fees, let alone for hotels, meals, and gasoline. A couple days later, a friend reached out to Sallie: "Have you thought about starting a blog?" Her idea was simple. Sallie would write posts about her training and add a link on her Facebook page. Her friend put a donation button on the blog, and in a matter of weeks, Sallie and Esco's first show season was paid for. The donations totaled about $600, just enough to pay Sallie's entry for six shows, two shows at three different venues. Sallie and Michael were broke, but Sallie was adamant that the donated money be used for shows only, and Michael was satisfied with that stipulation. If Esco needed a curry comb, he didn't get one. If there was no food in the house, Sallie wouldn't touch the donated money. People gave this money to me for show season, she thought. That's what it's for.

Osinski had given Sallie an important goal for the coming season. She would compete at training level—the lowest—and she hoped to "break 60," or score at least 60 percent on a dressage test. While no rider has ever scored a perfect test, those who break 60 have shown that they've mastered their level. It was a formidable goal for any horse woman, and a significant goal for someone recovering from a traumatic brain injury. And Sallie would be competing on the back of her highly spirited but inexperienced horse. She felt grateful that Osinski would be helping her and Esco throughout the entire show season. She considered it an incredible gift.

CHAPTER 15
CONSEQUENCES RUN DEEP

So while Sallie's work with Esco and Osinski was now paying a dividend and taking her to the next level of challenge that she yearned for, the impact of her injury and the years of challenge with her recovery were producing more unintended consequences at home. 2011 had been a year when her relationship with Chayce had changed and become strained. He was more distant and less communicative with Sallie. They had always enjoyed a close relationship, but it was evident to her that something had changed. It was out of concern that Sallie took her son to Doctor Monson. He had done so much for her, and it was her hope that if he needed to unload the pain he was carrying, he could do it with the doctor.

On their first visit Sallie introduced Chayce to Doctor Monson, then explained that she thought her son was struggling and saddened. She also said that he had been staying in his room most every day and no longer joined the family for most any occasion. Sallie concluded by saying that she thought Chayce was depressed. Doctor Monson listened intently and turned to ask Chayce a question when the boy said, "See….this person right here" while pointing to Sallie. "This is not my mom. This is the mom I raised. My real mom is dead." Sallie stayed silent, but Doctor Monson asked Chayce, "The mom you raised?" Chayce answered, "Yes. After that accident, I raised my mom. I got her as toddler." Doctor Monson replied saying "Chayce, I can see where you feel that way, but she is still the same mom." Chayce did not waiver but replied, "You don't understand. My mom, before this one, was the alpha and omega, ok? Everyone loved her. Everyone respected her. People wanted to talk to her all the time because she was smart. Going somewhere with my mom, everyone knew her. Now all she is one big joke. No one in the family likes her anymore. My grandfather jokes about her all the time. How is it that she has a brain injury that caused her all this difficulty? No one believes it. All she does is sleep. She is tired all the time. She can't talk clear half the time. She is dizzy a lot.....and I hate her for it. I hate this mom. I want my old mom back. Even you would have liked her."

Sallie sat silent, her heart breaking for Chayce. She was not angered by what she heard, but instead, felt a wave of understanding and compassion for her son. Doctor Monson looked at Sallie and said "Why don't you have a seat in the waiting room so Chayce and I can talk." Sallie left the office. It was a long 45 minutes that followed while she considered what Chayce had said. While she understood why he felt the way he did, she was also consumed by the feeling that her injury had robbed her son of a part of his childhood. There was no self-pity in what she was feeling, just the pain induced by a reality found in how her injury had injured those around her. It was a different injury for sure, but their pain was just as real.

It was about 45 minutes later when Doctor Monson returned to the waiting room and asked Sallie to rejoin them in the office. As she entered the room, Sallie noticed that Chayce looked much relieved. Doctor Monson asked Chayce to take a seat in the waiting room while he talked to Sallie.

Once alone, Doctor Monson closed the door. "Sallie, if people ......adults that is, could only realize the agony they cause children, especially teenagers, when they speak out of arrogance and ignorance about an injury that cannot be seen. If they could actually see the pain they cause them. But too often they think they are actually helping the kid. You were very smart to bring him in. He does have things he needs to work out. Obviously the parent-child roles got reversed for a while. And, you already know that is hard on kids. I would like to see him once a week."

And that appointment became the starting point for yet another part of her recovery. Sallie would take Chayce to see Doctor Monson for the next three months. There was a lot to heal, and the healing came slowly. While their relationship started to show improvement, it would not be until Chayce graduated from high school that they would finally realize the full breadth of what they had once known.

2012

CHAPTER 16
RIDE THIS STRIDE

In the meantime February 17, 2012, the fourth anniversary of her accident was fast approaching. Osinski had given her hope of a new found confidence. She and Esco were slowly becoming a team. The relationship was still fragile between the two of them, but there was a relationship. The week leading up to the 17th, Osinski could see the tension in Sallie. It was clear on her rides on Esco. Her muscles were tightening with every ride. She was on the edge of shrinking back, or just merely hanging on in her life, and also in her riding. One morning in conversation, Sallie mentioned to Osinski, "Ugh! The anniversary is coming. I can feel it in my body. I get so, so" Osinski answered, "tense?" Sallie nodded in agreement. Sallie then looked at Osinski, "You know, this is the first year. 2011 is the first year I have actually been able to ride in February. And, so far I have ridden every single day." Osinski smiled and said, "Yes and that is why I think you should ride the 17th." Sallie thought for a moment, digesting it, "I think I will try. Just driving here will be hard, but I have to face the day, Osinski. If I can face that day, maybe it won't own me so much." Osinski realized in that very moment, without question, this would be emotionally hard for her but a personal victory that she very much needed. "I am out of town Judging that day, but I want you to ride. Have someone video it for you. I want to see it."

The next few days were getting a bit more intense. But she continued to practice living in the moment with her meditation routine at home and riding 'ride this stride' daily on Esco. The night before the 17th, Osinski sent her a text, "Have a great ride tomorrow!" The text was just what she needed for accountability. On the morning of February 17th 2012, she woke up and decided she would come out swinging to win the war so to speak. She got dressed quickly, started up her truck and drove with purpose and intent right down to the training facility. She had a march to her stride as she took all of Esco's tack out to the cross ties. Then she walked out to the paddock area to gather up Esco. "Hi son." she said as she put his halter on. She led him, while he proudly began to lick and chew, to the cross ties and began tacking him up. "I know Esco. I know. It's about you and me today. This ride is for us" she said softly.

The two walked out to the gate of the arena. Sallie looked in at the vacant 100x200 foot riding, thinking " it looks much bigger when no one else is here.' The young gal who was there to video stood quietly by the gate as Sallie took Esco to the mounting block. She walked up each step, tapping the sand off each toe. She shortened the reins, gave Esco a quick pat, took a deep breath, and mounted quickly. 'Ride this stride, this stride. The last 5 do not matter they are gone, the next 10 do not count they are not here.' were the words running through her mind. She gave Esco a quick tap with both legs, and away they went in the trot. Staying mentally present in every stride and physically riding in each stride, she could feel the power of Esco. It, to her, was an amazing feeling. She felt empowered riding each and every stride. She could hear Esco licking and chewing the bit as he was very focused on her cues. She gave him a pat on the neck while saying quietly "good boy, son!"

While at the short 100 foot end of the arena, she then knew it was time to ask for the canter. Mentally she knew it was time to ask for it, but her psyche was saying something different. She asked Esco to pick up the canter anyway. As she and Esco cantered the rest of the short side, the PTSD flash of him falling on her appeared. . As she and Esco approached the corner, another flash of Esco falling on her happened. She whispered from her gut, "I choose life!" While continuing to ride up the long 200 foot side of the arena while in the canter, another flash of him falling, rolling on her and crushing her appeared." With every single flash she answered, "I choose life!" It was a battle of life and death. The combination of Osinski's coaching and daily meditation gave her the skills to answer with such conviction while riding. Death was chasing her around that ring while riding. She had to stand up to it. The more she responded, "I choose life!" to the flashes, the more proud and intense Esco became. She could feel him become more focused in the canter and more at ease. In this very ride, the flashes of him falling ended. They ended and would never again return to that level. Nor would they happen when she drove. PTSD would always be there. But it would only be a whisper.

From upon Escogido's back, Sallie chose life. It was a win in life. This was the very day declaring suicide would never again be an option or come to mind again. She was stronger than the PTSD. She was stronger than all the fear. She was stronger than all the ignorance and arrogance with regard to lack of awareness with TBI's. This was the day, she knew she belonged and was strong enough to remain in the game of life. This was the day she truly became a leader of her life again.

The painful nerve damage, the cognitive deficits, the vision impairment, the swallowing and breathing issues, the fatigue and exhaustion, they just would become part of life. Riding alone for the video proved that. It was the hand that life dealt her. In 2012, the show season taught her how to navigate those losses. Osinski sent her another text, "Did you ride?" Sallie smiled as she sent a text back, "Yes!" Osinski responded in a text, "Woo-hoo! Good for you!"

The recognition of the personal accomplishment moved and empowered her soul. She felt she had come full circle. Things were coming together. She was entering her first show soon. Show season 2012 would test how she would respond to showing period. It was a testing phase of sorts. How much was too much simulation for her? How much was too much activity? How could she do with her lack of focus and the concentration deficits? How would she do under pressure with a TBI? Could she manage Esco with such deficits as nerve damage to a lower left leg she could not feel? It would be self-discovery testing her new found confidence and skill, and self-control.

During the first show, at FPEC, Sallie kept herself aware of the slightest indication that Escogido would become distracted. At the end of the arena was an open area. Sallie knew that Esco tended to spook there because of the sudden appearance of people and other horses. She worked to keep him very focused. At one point, she could tell he was going to break in the canter—that he was going to drop from the canter to the trot. Not wanting to lose points over that, Sallie brushed her whip against Esco's hide.

That set Esco off. He exploded into a temper tantrum and took off, stamping his feet in the canter. His hoof beats were so forceful that dirt flew from the ground. He wanted to fling Sallie out of the saddle. How dare she tap him in front of all these people!

Sallie had been right. She knew Esco, and she had been sure he was going to break in the canter. As he stormed across the arena, she kept her seat and rode him out. But she was fuming; Esco was behaving like a spoiled toddler. People at the end of the arena were clapping as Esco slowed and stopped. "Wow! That took some power to ride that out," the spectators told her. "He was really pounding. He sounded like a herd of buffalo running in here." The show staff took Esco under their care. It was standard practice to check the bit and make sure there was no blood and that no abuse had taken place.

While they were checking Esco, Sallie burned inside. People were complimenting her, but her frustration made her boil. She knew how well she and Esco could work together in lessons with Osinski. And this test was by far less than their best. Tears were starting to fill her eyes. Sallie was relieved to see Osinski's familiar face. "Sallie, come here." The familiar voice was soothing. "Walk with me to the barn," he said. "We can be upset with ourselves, Sallie. We mustn't ever be upset with the horse." "Well, he was a jerk—" "Well, I disagree," Osinski said. "We can ride better. We can always ride better, and you can ride better.Sallie still was not getting it. "But he was a jerk! I tapped him, and he—" "Sallie, we can blame ourselves," Osinski said. "Can we be upset we did not ride better, handle the horse in the situation better? Yes. But we cannot blame the horse." Holding back tears, Sallie asked, "But when does it stop?" "When does what stop? "Being upset with yourself?" Osinski chuckled and answered, "Well, it's dressage, Sallie. So never, really. We are all trying to do better. Each ride, each show. There is always something we can improve. How do you think you scored? Do you think it was a 60?" "Far from it," Sallie said. "Esco and I do much better in our lessons. That was a terrible test." "Well, I think you're going to be surprised," Osinski said gently. Sallie retrieved Esco and walked him to cool him down. Once he was settled, she went to look at the scores—hers was something to make her smile, 61.25 percent. Wahoo!

Once again, Sallie had to address her lack of funds. She had money for entry fees but nothing left to pay for Esco's board. The sponsor had helped her for a month, and after that, Sallie and Michael had sold a horse to pay for Esco's board for a niine months. Time had run out, and Esco still very much needed Osinski's attention. Osinski was in the habit of riding Esco four days a week to give him a thorough workout before Sallie got on him. Sallie and Esco were working well together as long as Osinski could train him.

Sometimes, when Osinski was called away to judge shows for a week or so, Sallie had Esco all to herself. If Osinski left on a Friday, Sallie could ride him on Saturday, but by Sunday, he'd still become too much horse for her to handle. He was smart enough to know he'd get the better of Sallie. She would longe him on Sunday, and by the time Osinski returned on Monday, Sallie would tell him Esco had become a "fire-breathing dragon." "OK, well I don't really think he's a fire-breathing dragon, I think he just needs good, honest work," Osinski would say. "Why don't you go bring him in next." Sallie would lead a fiery, exuberant Esco to him, and the trainer would laugh. "Well, Esco, you're ready to work, aren't you? OK, let's go!" And Osinski would challenge Esco mentally. As an FEI rider, Osinski knew the upper-level movements and could keep ahead of Esco's busy mind. If Esco wanted to play, Osinski turned his antics into a movement. Sallie imagined Osinski saying, "Oh, you want to do that? Well, here, let's just go ahead and counter-canter all the way around the entire arena four times. Hey, it's not my fault you changed leads like that. You're just going to keep on with it."

In 2012, Sallie and Esco were both better, but neither one was ready to stop training. If Sallie couldn't afford Esco's board, he'd have to come home with her, and she knew it would be only a matter of days before he was out of control. And if she couldn't control him, she'd have to sell him. The possibility was unthinkable. But it was real. Michael had told Sallie, "I'm sorry, honey, you'll have to bring him home."

Sallie carried her sadness with her to an appointment with her chiropractor. As she was getting an adjustment, she started crying. Sallie's chiropractor was a good fit for her needs—he was a neuroscientist in addition to a chiropractor, and he owned horses. He believed Sallie when she said dressage lessons were making her better, and he sympathized with her when she told him she'd have to bring Esco home.

Sallie was touched when he actually wiped the tears off her face. He said, "Well, you believe in miracles, Sallie Stewart, because you can create one in your life today." Sallie wasn't so sure. "What miracle? Are you kidding me?" she thought. She drove home, still feeling sad. "I'm facing having to sell Esco—again. Here we go again." Her hands were shaking when she logged on to Facebook. She had no intention of asking for donations—she felt people had been kind enough to her already. But she wanted to reach out. As she typed she thought "Believe in miracles, Sallie, you could create one in your life today. Well, please show me how." She posted it, then settled in for her usual nap. When she woke up, she brewed some coffee and strolled to her computer to check her Facebook page, which had exploded with responses.

"What?" "What happened?" "What do you need?" and "If anyone could create a miracle, it's you!" Sallie replied, telling her friends she'd have to bring Esco home, and that would mean selling him. She couldn't keep a horse she couldn't ride. Once they understood what Sallie needed, people showed their generosity. One woman offered to help and asked others to do the same. She followed up with a private message to Sallie and offered to pay the stable for a month's board. Another woman wrote, "I'm going to help you if I have to do this single-handedly." She paid the stable for several months' board. Sallie was in shock. She was receiving a substantial amount of help from people who didn't know her. These people wanted nothing from her in return. They simply asked Sallie to pay it forward when she could.

With Esco's board taken care of, Sallie could focus on show season. Osinski hauled Esco to Devon Wood, the site of her next show and a site so beautiful that she initially thought the name to be Dreamin'-Wood. Despite its beauty, Sallie made considerable sacrifice in order to compete. She had no money for a hotel, so she slept on the tack room floor in the stalls. The stalls were temporary portable shelters set up outdoors, and Sallie's bed was an old cot mere inches off the ground. During the show dates, a massive electrical storm moved through the area—and Sallie slept off her exhaustion right in the middle of it, surrounded by four horses and their equipment.

Not all of the other riders understood Sallie's situation. Some gave her odd looks and smirks. Their judgment didn't hinder Sallie. She knew why she was at that show and what it had cost to get there. Having to sleep on the tack room floor was nothing to her—her worst moment had happened already, when her grandfather had refused to give her a job or understand that Sallie had significant issues because of her TBI. She had already decided that she would chin-up and take whatever others might say or ignore it when people looked at her strangely. When the other riders went out to dinner, Sallie stayed behind. Meals out were too expensive, and in addition, she would become overstimulated in a restaurant. She was simply grateful to have the experience. She was still alive and was finally competing with the horse that she deeply loved. She was learning how much was too much stimulus, and how to establish boundaries. Sallie discovered she couldn't take in too much information or handle too many distractions. Her brain would become so overloaded she no longer knew where she was. That's what happened as she took her first test at Devon Wood.

The challenges were no less in the arena. Esco stumbled and the stumble allowed Sallie's focus dissolve. She forgot where she was in the test and completely checked out. She and Esco went off course, and Sallie didn't even know it. When the bell rang, she had absolutely no idea where she was in the test. The judge had to tell her what she had just ridden and what the next pattern was. She felt caught again in that time/space void, trying to find her bearings and trying to hear and see. When she finished the test, she wasn't really certain if she had ridden all the patterns. She felt out of sorts, her eyesight was fuzzy, and she was overcome with intense emotion. She later learned from Dr. Monson that her overloaded brain had shut itself off. In the middle of the confusion, Sallie saw Osinski sitting in the audience.

Osinski, his face, his voice…suddenly everything came clear to Sallie. "OK, I'm in Oregon, I'm in Devon Wood, I'm in a show. I'm riding and I need to go back in. I need to listen to the judge. This is where I'm at." Sallie thought she psyched herself out because she had heard one of the judges was tough. As she rode, she had been thinking Oh my God, she's watching me ride. Oh my God, I'm done now.

Sallie didn't know whether the judge was tough or not, but she did know her own thinking defeated her before she walked into the show ring. Still, going off course was unbelievable to her. Afterward, Osinski met her at the end of the ring, clearly disappointed. "Good boy, Esco, you did exactly what your mom told you to do," he said. And he was right. Esco had been a very good boy. He listened to Sallie's every cue. Even when Sallie had given him an incorrect riding aid, Esco listened to her and was very obedient. After her poor test, Sallie couldn't talk to anybody. She rode off on Esco, then came back to the tack room crying. Osinski joined her there. Like any good coach, Osinski knew he would not be able to help Sallie until she had calmed down. "I'll take care of Esco," he said. "Sallie, it's good to see you're hard on yourself. I'm happy to see this. And it's good to see that you take this seriously. But you have got to leave this emotion. Now, go to your car, go for a walk, do whatever you need to do. Get out of the emotion and come back when you're done." When Sallie came back, he told her, "You went off course and that's OK."

The next day at the show was a huge one for Sallie and Esco. She rode better and stayed on course, and while still disappointed in what happened on the first day of riding, she reinforced her will not to let what was out of her control take her down. When Sallie returned from Devon Wood, she called her grandfather. She intended to thank him "for being an asshole." She wanted to tell him that she'd brushed off the looks and comments she had received from other riders—that she'd been tough because of him. However, she didn't get the chance. "I'm on the way to the hospital right now," he told her as soon as he picked up the phone. One of his employees had been in an accident, and he was lucky to be alive. Like Sallie, the employee had suffered a traumatic brain injury. In the months to come, Sallie's grandfather would watch his employee go through the same long and laborious process that Sallie had endured. Through no fault of his own, grandpa would come to understand what a TBI was and how it would change any person it touched.

In the meantime, Sallie and Esco were off to Donida. Sallie had enough money for the entry fee, and because it was close by, one tank of gas. During the Donida show, she stayed at the home of a friend who lived 20 minutes away. Her friend provided meals, and Sallie watched her fuel gauge as she drove to and from the show site that weekend. She felt that she had asked for enough from others, and she refused to ask for more, even when she did not have enough money for a cup of coffee. She was overwhelmed with gratitude for the Facebook friends who had helped her at a time when her family wouldn't give her a job. Esco was in high spirits too.

The first day at Donida, Sallie brought Esco out and put him on the longe line. Esco was bouncing, bucking, and snorting. At that point, the horse had caught on that he was in a competition, and he was sure he needed to perform. He needed to lift his legs much higher than any other horse; he needed to go much faster than any other horse. He needed to show how proud he was. He needed to be the best. Sallie understood. Just as she needed to find her zone that first year, Esco needed to find where his center was. "Esco, you're not supposed to jump higher or run faster," Sallie told him. "You don't need to do that—you just have to be the best you." Once she finished warming him up on the longe line, she tacked him up so Osinski could ride him. Esco kept up the silliness throughout Osinski's ride, until the trainer had had enough.

Once out of the show ring, Osinski got right off Esco and handed Sallie the reins. "Here" he said with all deliberateness. Sallie rode Esco for her class a couple hours later. Her score was in the 50s, not as high as she would have liked, but for her, showing wasn't about winning. She was learning what she and Esco were capable of. And she was learning that emotion could not rule her life. Life wasn't fair, and she had to accept what her abilities were now. Focus was harder. Concentration was harder, and getting back on target was harder than it had ever been. She was learning not only how to accept her new shortcomings, but how to navigate them.

The next day at Donida, Esco was bouncing around on the longe line as Sallie warmed him up—acting like his tail is on fire, she thought. She tried to calm him down, but Esco was so invigorated and excited that he pranced and skipped through his warm-up. Sallie tacked him up and handed him to Osinski. "Esco, no cartwheels!" the trainer said. They needn't have worried. Esco completed a beautiful first-level test under Osinski's guidance. Esco was so compliant and so obedient that he drew a little crowd. Sallie watched her spirited horse make every move and every stride just as Osinski asked him to do. The test moved her to tears. Esco was finally focused on his job. He was finally at peace with his place in his life. That day would be different. Osinski and Esco scored in the high 60s, averaging over 68 percent for the season, and Sallie was proud of her bright, copper-colored horse and grateful to her coach.

As busy as Sallie's life had become with Esco, those who had joined Sallie's journey along the way were not lost. Michael remained a quiet but steady force behind the scenes. He continued to balance the daily family and farm routines that often consumed hours each day with his job some 40 miles away. By then the couple's financial problems had relaxed somewhat, aided by the reorganization of their debt. With the help of friends and supporters, they were finally able to balance the costs associated with training and competition with their family expenses. She kept her Facebook friends and supporters up to date on her progress by posting her scores after every show. She had set out to break 60 with a TBI, and she had done it at her first show. With all the deficits Sallie dealt with as a result of the TBI, she was learning the art of navigating her life. And she had learned a lot about herself and Esco—things she would never have learned if they had not entered shows. Sallie could now set boundaries and take care of herself, even during a competition.

While Osinski observed Sallie's progress, he also saw significant holes in her riding. Sallie expected to leave training level, the lowest level, behind her, and compete in her next show season at first level. Osinski wouldn't allow that. "I want you to do training level again," he said. "Sallie, there are skills in riding that, if not fully understood at training and first level, will follow a horse and rider all the way to the upper levels. Esco deserves better. You deserve better. When we do right by the horse, Sallie, everyone involved wins." Sallie was crushed. She held back tears. Osinski was right, and she knew it was hard news for him to deliver. She also knew he was honest. She had broken 60 in her first show of the season, but not again. She had only made it to the high 50s. And she had worked for that tremendously hard, riding Esco six days a week and taking lessons four days a week. To know she had to come back out at training level after she had worked so hard felt like defeat. Nevertheless, Sallie didn't want any holes in her riding. And she deeply loved Esco. She had to do right by Esco. It was her love for Esco that gave her determined soul perseverance. She knew she would have to try harder.

The spring of 2012 Sallie brought a renewed challenge in the form of a nagging injury. Sallie was still unable to connect her mind to the left side of her body. If Osinski told her to go left, she went right. He could not get her to turn left unless he pointed her in that direction. For the most part, Sallie rode with the right side of her body. Esco, though, was left-side dominant. Once Osinski recognized Esco's left-side dominance. He realized he had to get Sallie to move her left side. That's what they worked on in preparing for the 2013 show season. He challenged Sallie. "If I don't see your left leg moving, I'm going to walk out of this arena," he would tell her. In Sallie's mind, she was kicking her left leg with all her might, but the leg made only a tiny wiggle. Whenever she was sure her leg was extended straight out the side of her hip joint, the movement was only a slight lift. However hard Sallie tried to move that leg, it barely responded.

As time and training progressed, Osinski would not lower his standards or cut Sallie any slack. "You can do this. You can". Every time he raised the bar, Sallie kept reaching. Her ability to move her left leg improved, and so did her riding. More important, the lessons carried over to all aspects of her life. Sallie learned how to navigate her deficits and her shortcomings on Esco's back with Osinski coaching her every step of the way. When Esco acted up, Osinski told Sallie not to feed into his drama. "I don't care that he is doing this, that, or the other. You keep your hands quiet, you use your leg, you say, 'Come on, Esco, move forward.' You just stay solid in what you know."

The lesson helped Sallie stand up to those who didn't want to understand her limitations. If she had to refuse an invitation, for example, she wouldn't allow someone to guilt or shame her into attending. She could understand that was their drama, not hers. When necessary, she learned to say, "I'm sorry you don't understand. I'm going to end this conversation now."

"You must own what you know, Sallie," Osinski told her over and over. Sallie began to set clear boundaries for herself, for Esco, and for friends and family members.

2013

CHAPTER 17
YOU MUST OWN WHAT YOU KNOW

As her skills and physical abilities improved, so did her confidence. She would need all of that for the 2013 show season, especially since Osinski had decided he would no longer show Esco, it was now time to raise the bar for herself. "I'll help you in the warm-up, and if you need me to, I'll get on him, and I'll be there for you, but you're going to do this now," he said. "OK, that's good," Sallie said. She also felt it was time to stand on her own. She and Osinski had agreed she would compete at training level again. And to keep challenging herself, she would try first level as well.In May 2013, Sallie and Esco returned to Donida. For this show, Osinski had offered to ride Esco first to get him warmed up. But Esco was so relaxed he seemed to be almost asleep. Sallie could tell, that if she worked with him on the longe line, she would wear him out before the competition started. Esco was in a good mood and didn't need to shake off any excess energy. This was a new Esco for Sallie. He clearly remembered the show grounds, was relaxed, and had nothing to prove. So Sallie simply tacked him up and offered the reins to Osinski. "Did you longe him first? You've longed him and everything and he's good?" the trainer said. "No, he doesn't need to be longed today," Sallie told him. "He needs to be longed." "No, really, there isn't going to be enough horse if we're both going to ride him." Osinski knew Esco, and he knew what a handful he could be and had been for two years. He told her to "go buck him out," meaning that he wanted her to ride Esco as he let off steam by bouncing, bucking, and acting out. "OK," Sallie said. She knew Esco would remain calm. She climbed up the mounting block. "Get down," Osinski said. He went up the mounting block, took the reins, and said, "All right, Mr. Esco, let's go." The trainer gave Esco a brief warm-up. "OK," he told Sallie, "he's being very honest today. Just give him a light workout and put him up." Sallie's confidence soared. She had read Esco right, and her coach had confirmed it.

The next day was blazing hot. Sallie, dressed in an old-style wool coat, shirt, breeches, boots, and helmet, felt very uncomfortable. In the warm up ring, Sallie's breathing turned into an issue. She could not inhale, and she could not exhale, nor could she swallow. It was a storm of symptoms that was happening more and more frequently. Michael was with her, and he ran to get her inhaler from the truck. She took a much-needed puff seconds before the bell rang, signaling it was time to enter the ring.

Esco entered the arena and came down the centerline. Esco powerfully and boldly blew down the centerline in the trot.. As she led Esco down their first single loop, she remembered more of Osinski's words: "And where's left bend? Show me left bend." Sallie and Esco rode around the short end of the arena, and just before she instructed Esco to pick up left canter, Sallie heard, "And he does not get to break in the canter." They came across the diagonal for the canter-to-trot transition and the trot-to-walk transition. "Loose rein, do not let him jig!" Sallie gathered up her reins and used leg aids to ask Esco for the trot, making the first right bend for the single loop. "Play the rein! Play the rein! He does not get to come above that bit!" They came down the long side in the canter and made the turn for the right-lead canter 20-meter circle. "No breaking! Don't you dare let him break in the canter He does not get to trot!" Sallie asked Esco for his stretchy circle in the trot. "With your hands you tell him to reach downward, forward and into your hands." Sallie and Esco came down the centerline to X and halt salute. It was an easy score of 60. Osinski had been right to work them another year.

Sallie was to show in the first-level class that same day. The heat was getting to her, and she was losing energy and focus. Osinski could see her exhaustion. He took Michael aside. "She looks tired." "She is tired," Michael replied. "Should I coach her? Do you think she will listen to me?" "Yeah, I would coach her," Michael said. "If you give her some support, it would probably mean the world to her. But just one or two things—don't give her too much." Osinski got Sallie's attention. She welcomed his familiar voice. "Sallie, look at me," he said. "Find your zone. Clear your head. Breathe. Focus on your core. Your hands are erratic and shaking. Quiet your hands. Good. Sallie breathed deeply. "OK. Do I have to ride with this whip?" "No, there's no rule that you have to ride with that whip." Sallie dropped it. Thinking about her hands helped her focus despite the heat and her exhaustion, and Esco was able to perform well. The judges awarded them a score of 58.

She had to cancel her participation the next day at Donida, as two tests a day were too much for her brain to process. She was absolutely exhausted and very slow moving. After the Donida show, Sallie was exhausted for the next two days. She had to go to the Dr, she simply was not recovering. During the doctor's appointment, he was firm with her she would have to cut her physical activity back. Her adrenals were fatigued, and it was cut back on her daily physical activity or go on steroids daily. She had a serious choice to make. With tears down her cheeks, she drove to the training facility, to deliver the news of her health. She was so grateful for Osinski's guidance and coaching, but she was so sad, she would no longer be able to tack and groom for him. She would lose a sense of community, too, that she gained at the facility. She enjoyed the people who boarded their horses there, and especially those who worked there keeping the grounds, fences and buildings maintained. When she shared the news with Osinski, she did fight back tears welling in her eyes, "It's the Addison's' Disease. It has reared its head back up." she said choking back tears. "I have secondary Addison's. So it is not active all the time. My doctor said to cut back my physical activity, or I will have to be placed on steroids for life." As she whipped the tears. "You have done so much for Esco and for me. I don't want you to think I am being selfish and just running out on you. Or like I used you or something."

Osinski looked up at her kindly and with deep compassion as he said, "isn't it sad , Sallie, that in the English language and culture we do not have just a single word that means, 'Take care of yourself.' It is ok that you take care of yourself Sallie. You don't want to be on steroids if you have a choice in it. I don't think you are being selfish at all. " As she stood there in the tack room, whipping tears away from her cheek He gave her a fatherly hug. "You take care of you, Sallie" he told her. She asked "Can I still haul in for my lesson once a week?" Osinski nodded and said, "Of course. I will have to work you in. So if you can be patient and shoot me a text, so I can fit you in....?" She nodded in agreement that she could and would faithfully keep in close contact.

This was a big step for Sallie and for Esco. He would now be home at her farm. The routine of him being longed for 30 minutes to let him get his expelled energy out, then handing him over to Osinski, was done.. Sallie had to be the one to get on him to ride. Osinski would no longer be training him four times a week. It had to all be done by Sallie. Faithfully and earnestly she worked Esco daily six days a week. After each ride she collapsed for a few hour nap.   Slowly, she regained some physical endurance.   With the continued homework, she and Esco were in good form at their next show at FPEC, where they earned 61 on the training-level ride and 57 on the first-level ride. Her scores over the next shows increased in tiny increments: 61, 62, 63. The numbers meant less to Sallie than her ability to make progress. She had learned how to remain emotionally balanced, even during the times she struggled with her body's neurological and cognitive deficits. She had learned "own what you know" and "don't feed into anyone else's drama."

Their next show, at Whidbey, tested Sallie's patience and sportsmanship. She and about six other riders were on their horses in the arena when another rider entered the arena and guided her horse too close to the other riders, running them out of the enclosure. That rider wasn't showing that day, but was moving her horse so close to the other riders that it was scaring them out of the ring. Sallie, who had a class to prepare for, held her ground. She was concerned—the rider's behavior was dangerous, and Sallie could not risk another fall on Esco. "You're not pushing me around ", Sallie thought. The rider taunted her: "Is this close enough? How's this now?" She cut directly in front of Sallie, and Esco could feel her hand pass his body. Fed up, Sallie told the person at the gate that the other rider was bumping her into the wall. "Would you like me to get a TD?" the person said.

Sallie had no idea if talking to a technical delegate, an official who made sure no cheating or abuse took place during a competition, would be acceptable. As a student of Mike Osinski, she felt she needed to show proper behavior that would not reflect badly on her coach. She chose not to pursue it. But Esco was angry, and he took it out on Sallie as they entered the ring. As soon as Sallie had saluted the judges and they had rung the bell, signaling for her to begin, Esco showed his fury. He rooted so hard on the bridle in the canter he was ripping Sallie's entire body out of the saddle with his massive neck. She looked at one of the judges. "Scratch," Sallie said. "Good call," the judge replied. Sallie knew she had avoided an explosive show of anger from Esco.

Esco calmed down for the Summervale show, where he and Sallie earned a 63. They were set to return to Donida for the second show of 2013.

Earlier that year, Esco had developed chronic obstructive pulmonary disorder, and the veterinarian had put him on steroids, which had the effect of making him very agitated. The moment he entered the ring at Donida, the fire-breathing dragon was once again ignited. Osinski had coached her how to ride Esco through his tantrums. Sallie knew how to handle her dragon. Instead of getting irritated with him, she dropped her anger and stayed focused. Esco behaved and did everything Sallie asked, even though he wanted to jump out of the ring. She could feel him working under her saddle, and she could stay ahead of him when he wanted to do something other than what she had asked him to do. She made judicious use of her spur and whip to keep Esco in line when he wanted to argue with her.

Sallie began to think of Esco as the best kind of antagonizer—one that forced her to grow. She could ride him, and Osinski often said that if she could ride Esco, she could ride any horse. She had also learned to distinguish the difference between something she did wrong and Esco's emotional behavior. And while she wanted to perform well at shows, she saw the value of her worst rides, the ones that taught her the most valuable lessons.

Life, like dressage shows, has good rides and tough ones. Sallie was learning to hold on to a sense of peace with every challenge she met and every show she attended. She brought Esco to FPEC a couple days before her show to let him calm down before they entered the ring. It was a good decision, and Sallie and Esco had a great ride. Sallie felt she had earned the right to be in that ring with her horse. Her hard work had paid off, and she was at peace with herself. She knew, with deep conviction, that no one was going to shove her around or boss her around anymore—in any ring.

As she was coming home from the successful show, her grandfather called to tell her she should stop messing around with horses. That made Sallie horribly angry and sad. She had yet to make her peace with him. That was a relationship that she felt was forever broken. In so many ways she loved her grandfather. She had always looked up to him and had the highest respect for him. Throughout her life he had been a mentor of sorts to her. But since her accident, the two just did not get along. A few weeks later her Grandfather would call again. As Sallie saw the words, "Gramps' appear on her cell phone screen, she uttered "Oh shit" to herself. Her guts churned as she answered the phone "Hello!" He immediately said "Good morning. Hey are you up yet? I thought you lived on a farm, you should be up by 4 am." Sallie was tired and fed up with the last few years of his antagonizing. "Yes grandpa I am just a lazy fucking asshole who got up at 7:00 am now what do you want?" There was a brief pause, before her grandfather sarcastically said, "Now is that anyway to talk to your grandfather?' She fired back in a strong but soft tone, "I...I don't know how to talk to you anymore." His antagonistic banter was about to begin and before he could respond she fired off, "Gramps, does my life matter? Does my life count to you at all?" there was silence.

She could hear him take a controlled sigh and in his compassionate voice that used to be familiar, and a tone she had not heard from him in years, he said, "You know there were words said, I wish I could take back. I watch Gill, after his accident, and I now see the similarities. How do you know what a TBI is until you have one I guess? I have been very hard on you, and for that I am truly sorry. I know you regressed. I watched him do the same thing. I watch him really struggle at times. He deeply feels he was responsible. But, shit happens. Sallie, shit happens. You did not cause the accident. Shit just happens. I am glad you are alive, and I love you honey." The words meant something and nothing at the same time for Sallie. It was a lot to process. She was agitated, and in some ways felt it was too little, too late for this apology. On the other hand she welcomed the conversation as she loved her grandfather and always had. She knew she had to forgive.

CHAPTER 18
EMBRACING THE LESSON

Osinski was aware of the conversation with her grandfather and her feelings. As they wound down the 2013 season and began training for 2014, he began to nudge Sallie to forgive her grandfather. He would ask, "Have you forgiven him yet?" "Yeah," Sallie said, but Osinski wasn't convinced. "You need to forgive him." Every so often Osinski would bring it up again. "Have you forgiven him yet?" "I'm working on it. I'm working on it." A few weeks later: "Have you forgiven? How's that forgiving going?" "It's coming," Sallie told him. "Forgiveness, I have learned comes in layers." "Good for you."

Then one day, as Sallie was riding Esco at home, she realized her anger was gone. She texted Osinski: "Hey! I forgive him. I totally forgive him." At their next lesson, Osinski said, "Good for you for forgiving him. What made you do it?" "You provoked the thought," Sallie said. "And really, I didn't want to be angry, ugly, and bitter. And I was getting really bitter. And I don't want to be that. That's just not me." "No," he agreed. "That's not you."

The next time her grandfather called, it was to tell Sallie that he was about to undergo a five-way bypass. Sallie was grateful that she could be completely present for him, not angry or vengeful. "I couldn't believe my grandfather had a five way by pass," Sallie told Osinski at their next lesson. "That was so sad for him. Thank you for encouraging me to forgive." It had been a long and difficult journey for Sallie's grandfather, but their relationship, which had once been close, was finally restored!

Mother's Day weekend in 2014 arrived with stormy weather that turned the dressage arena at Donida into a flooded pool. On the morning of her dressage test, Sallie looked over the arena with a sense of calm. Her arena at home was outdoors, and to manage her TBI symptoms, Sallie rode Esco, rain or shine, six days a week. The ankle-deep lake in front of her did not disturb her in the least. She and Esco were ready. It had rained inches that night. The show rings all outdoors were full of water. Esco was hesitant in wanting to trot or canter through all that water. Horses have no depth perception. Sallie could feel his hesitation, and with her "leadership' energy, Esco gave right in to Sallie and gave her his full trust. to guide him through a surface he couldn't see—one that was uneven and full of holes made by the other horses' hooves. The steady rain would soak their coats and make it harder for both of them to see. The horses that had been taking their tests all morning had spooked, and several had jumped into the air or tried to leap out of the ring.

Sallie entered that ring with the Osinski' words in her head, "You must own what you know Sallie."   X halt salute. She smiled at the Judge as she cued Esco on to a rising trot. As she asked Esco to track left, she heard the words, "Why does he get to come above the bit! Play that rein." As Esco began to move, someone popped open an umbrella. Before Esco could stop, she heard, "Keep him moving! I don't care if a bird flew in and pecked him on the end of his nose! He does not get to look around."

Coming across the diagonal in the lengthened trot she heard, "Now that you've found your confidence, can you lose it again? Yes. We keep it by maintaining our boundaries." During their leg yields she heard, "Is that a 6? Or an 8? Well then make them an 8!" During their stretchy circle, she heard "you feel his mouth keep the contact, you say, you keep hold of your momma's hand". At the 15 meter canter circle she heard, "Don't you quit! You quit riding, and he breaks in the canter. Don't you dare quit." During the canter single loop she heard, "Ride this stride! The last 5 are gone, the next 10 are not here. Ride this stride." Later, during the lengthened canter she heard, "Be the leader this horse needs and deserves you to be!" Finally, she was to the closing curtain. Coming up the centerline she heard, "You count! You matter! " and X halt salute. The voice inside her said "Esco counts! Esco, he does matter!" She smiled a soul felt smile and generously praised Esco for bravely trusting her and following her lead. He was the horse who chose her, the horse who chose his coach, and united all of them in humanity.

SALLIE A. STEWART

Sallie and Esco continue to compete at rated shows. Coach Mike Osinkski has committed to continue coaching them over the next several years until they reach the Grand Prix, the highest level of dressage in the U.S.

AFTERWORD

As we make our journey through life, everyone experiences some adversity. In her journey, Sallie experienced, and still experiences, ongoing adversity. As she reached out to others in her blog and through Facebook, she apparently struck a chord in many, who like her, faced, or knew others who faced, extreme adversity in various forms. How many have considered suicide, or just "given in" and given up in their circumstances? Perhaps Sallie's story struck a chord in many because hers is a story of perseverance, courage, set-backs, and recovery. Many of her Facebook friends asked her to tell her story because they were inspired by her efforts to continue to move forward in spite of many road blocks and many disappointments. Who among us has not thought about, at some truly low point, the possibility of suicide, or chosen to finally face ourselves, accept who we are, and continue to move forward face our challenges and overcome them, to find new reasons to live, and new successes in meeting challenge after challenge.

This book is a tribute to many, who reached out to support Sallie in meeting her challenges in so many ways. Whether it was a husband or a son, also challenged by her injuries, or others who saw in her something of themselves and reached out to teach, or to offer financial support, this story truly is about the miracle of humanity at its finest. It is also a blue-print for others to follow who face tragic circumstances. Additionally, it is a call to all of us to be accepting, and kind, and encouraging, and to lift each other up, rather than to judge or criticize. Most of us know someone who needs, if nothing else, unbiased acceptance, and help can be as simple as truly listening, rather than judging or criticizing from some safe, yet distant position of observation. Help can come in many forms. Sallie's story speaks to the humanity available to each of us to tap. It speaks to the goodness in us and pleads with us to reach out to make life better by offering ourselves, however we can, to pick ourselves up and "Try".

Pamela Krueger

Made in the USA
San Bernardino, CA
11 January 2016